Holosophy:
Exploring the Kosmic Code
the Archetypal Order of the Universe

by
Robert Thomas

The Holosophy Foundation Press

Dedication:

To all who helped ... but mostly

JSJ, LL, KF, DE, JT, PGT, ET, BT, NHT, MG, KM, CM,
ACW, PR, A&EM, JM, JLM, AC, RS, JJ, K&JS, JDS, FF,
LW, JC, SR, PL, R&PN, LS,

... and of course to my parents and
theirs who provided my most recent
vessel and port of entry

*"It is not the length of the life,
but the depth of the life..."*
In Memoriam, Jennifer St. John

Copyright 2018 by Robert Thomas

All rights reserved.

No part of this publication may be reproduced, stored in a retrieval system, or
transmitted in any form by any means, electronic, photocopying or otherwise
without the prior written permission of the publisher:
The Holosophy Foundation Press

Library of Congress Cataloging-in-Publication Data
Thomas, Robert

First Edition
(Volume II)
2018

The Holosophy Foundation
Holosophyfoundation.com

Holosophy and the Holosophy colophon are registered trademarks
Graphic design and editing by RT, executed by Tom White

Holosophy; Seminal Definition:
Holosophy incorporates and is essentially the study of 3 fundamental concepts: *Holon*: a nonmaterial, self-generated unit of consciousness with restorable and expandable ability and awareness. *Holos:* Greek; whole, entire; also that cognitive essence which is the source of whole*ness;* qualia; or reification. *Holism:* concisely summarized by Aristotle, "The whole is greater than the sum of its parts" (Modern term introduced by J. Smuts, 1946)

EXPLORING the KOSMIC CODE:

the Archetypal Order of the Universe

*Holon: (Greek: holos, 'whole') a non-material source unit of consciousness; an autonomous self-generating individuality; a spiritual agency, with the capacity to postulate (conceptually actualize) and perceive (have sustained awareness, control, and optimization of its actualizations) ... and with the cognitive capacity to combine conceptuality into gestalts, or creatively unified elements of a perceived reality

The Kosmic Domain Matrix

see back cover for full color version.

Nota Bene:

It is suggested that the reader make annotations to record queries, *disagreements*, ancillary *definitions*, comments or references helpful in discussing and the *productive de*-constructing of the text … since the present volume is also intended to be used as a text in a Holosophy seminar and as a dialogue, or selective tutorial, supporting workbook … in which case it may also serve as a useful memorandum or "case-book" of personal progress.

In this, as in *previous and any future volume*, the editors suggest that the reader honestly reflect on each quotation and/or reference, to seek cognitive access into productive introspection or a dialoguing opportunity … and to consult in a playfully diligent manner the contextual reference works[*] that frame *any* insights hidden in our humbly eclectic "wisdom" presentation.

---

[*]See Appendices and List of Publications

The world was not to be put in order; the world is order incarnate. It is for us to put ourselves in unison with this order...
—Henry Miller, author

"Each of us literally chooses, by his way of attending to things, what sort of a universe he shall appear to himself to inhabit."
— William James

"What is word knowledge but a shadow of wordless knowledge."
—Kahlil Gibran

"When I use a word," Humpty Dumpty said ...
"It means just what I choose it to mean—neither more nor less."

"The question is," said Alice, *"Whether you can make words mean so many different things?"*

"The question is, said Humpty Dumpty, *Which is to be Master?"*
—Lewis Carroll

"If actual conceptual knowing is confused with symbolized pictured knowing, then any symbol alone can command and compel any attached meaning and behavior."
—Holosophic Tenet

"What is lost in the (computer) simulation of cognitive behavior is the distinction between Syntax and Semantics."
—John Searle

"Even 'this' may be a case of mistaken identity."
—Master Dignaga, 830 AD

"Life's basic purpose is the joyous and transformative display of its innate capacities enroute to an ultimate Kosmic revelation."
—Holosophy precept

Upaya ... ('skillful means') is necessary for the transformation, and then ... the tranquil abiding of consciousness...
Excerpt: Buddhist text

Dialoguing simply removes fixed sub-rational significances from a past location, domain, or activity so that it can be re-familiarized, and used, without post traumatic-effect, as a part of the Kosmic playing field.
Holosophic Tenet

In this (subatomic) world of moving things, you can imagine it is something like a great game of chess, played by the Gods ... with something occasionally like castling going on.
-R. Feynman, physicist

Preface

The contents of this volume have been compiled from the author's collected lectures, articles, recorded dialogues and seminar materials spanning many years to the present. The information has been extensively revised, updated and expanded to achieve some degree of developmental coherence and continuity to maximize its logical development and comprehensibility.

In fact, this work was *designed* to accommodate a broad range of study *and* consulting applications—first as a seminar program manual; next, as a guiding philosophical text, coordinated with training drills and transformative exercises, to assist personal study and counseling. Finally, including the quotations which were selected from eclectic wisdom-sources and are intended to stimulate dialogue, and perchance, even elicit a chuckle or two! The hope is that the concepts and data presented will ultimately emerge "whole" and intact, despite *any* deficiencies of style or presentation which are, of course, the sole responsibility of the author.

-RT

EXPLORING the KOSMIC CODE:

Table of Contents:

Introduction	1
Part I: Exploring the Kosmic Code	11
Part II: Causation & Responsibility	51
Part III: Kosmic History and the Primal Mechanism of Sub-Rationality	76
Part IV: Sub-Rational Synonyms	96
Sub-Rational Synonyms (selected list)	103
Holosophy Terms in General Use	105
Compendium	106
Index of Appendices	111

"Perfection" must include the innate capacity for imperfection ...
- Anonymous

This brief introduction will assume the readers' basic familiarity with Holosophy as a subject, more fully explained in Volume I of this series. We will attempt to set the stage for the complex discussion of inter-domain causation and the "blaming" analysis to follow. This is not easy material and the reader is invited to proceed with an earnest but light-hearted diligence.

Introduction

Our representation of the Kosmos displayed* on page iv is in the tradition of the Mandala (Sanskrit: circle). In various spiritual traditions, mandalas may be used symbolically to focus and direct attention to a primal *sacred meaning space*, as an aid to increased contemplative awareness of an ultimate Source or Ground of all existence. In ordinary usage, the mandala has become, generally, a term for any grid, matrix, plan, et al., that represents the totality of existence, metaphysically, ... and which contains the *universal forms*, that, with appropriate contemplation, reveal from within, the innately disposed structure, meaning, and logical order of the *manifest* Kosmos.

The mandalic diagram symbolizes this basic structure, immanent order, and thematic domains of the Kosmic code, matrix, or actual pattern of existence. It captures the functional integrity and interactive aspects of the eight life-game domains, as follows:

First, the larger golden outer circle represents the 8th domain, the infinite potentiality which encompasses and grounds all other domains. The center is the mathematical unit of meaning for the quantum wave-form superimposed over the ancient Yin-Yang

---

*See back cover for full color rendition.

Tell me, where dwell the thoughts ... till thou call them forth?
  - Wm. Blake, poet

symbol, together representing the primal *reifying*[*] capacity of the 7th domain which radiates out to actualize domains 1-6. The arrows are variable in size and color to represent both the comparative degree of endowed order, and the implicit presence of *all* domains within each.

The central Yin-Yang symbol combined with the quantum wave-function and the "Golden Ratio" represents a primary and functional symbolic synthesis of the epistemic and ontic aspects of reality. The wave-function is placed more properly on the 7th domain since it symbolizes *potential* or possibility, and is not *real* until made consensually manifest as 6th domain, i.e., the collapse from wave-form into particulate "substance" through *conscious specification* (observation). The triadic symbology, the dynamic logic of projected eventuation (Be, Do, Have), the plus-minus duality of Yin-Yang, the golden mean of Cosmic proportionality, combine as a *consciousness directed formativeness, projected* by the 7th domain, and encompassed, as is *All*, by the 8th. Holosophy re-visions a profound *Kosmic*^{**} order in the universe. The Source of this order stands innate and independent of the manifest cosmic existence that is projected from it.

This Source of Kosmic order, which we call the *actual pattern of existence,* has been the subject of mystical and metaphysical contemplation since the most ancient of times. The early vedantic mandalas were intended to be a kind of cartography of potential universal form, and the potentiality of an emergent cosmic

---

*The word "reify" is used in Holosophy to mean the process of giving innate, non-material concepts, substance and perceptual reality, i.e., "*ideas* made *flesh*" or given "local habitation and a name" as Shakespeare beautifully describes it.

** Kosmos: an ancient Greek term used by Pythagoras to refer to the *entire* universe in all of its multi-dimensionality, i.e. spiritual, mental, emotional and *physical* ... as contrasted with "Cosmos" in its modern usage which refers *only* to the physical realm. This implies that the word is misplaced in the 6th domain and excludes the 7th and 8th.

> *The Qubit, because of its entangled multi-dimensional quantum capacities, more effectively simulates (as an informing symbol) the infinite conceptual context-potential of consciousness, than the mere "bit."*
> — Holosophic Tenet

pattern (code). These anticipated Plato's idea that *all* perceptible *things* derive from immaterial *thought forms*, and our common experience is an imperfect reflection of those ideal forms. These initially *pure* potentials were then made mundane by Aristotle's "entelechy"—a *dynamic eventuality,* or "*natures* that persist," but without any ultimate *non*-physical aspect or source.

By contrast, Plato's eternal *Ideas* are not just general concepts but are the innate prototypes of *all* particular and manifest things. These transcendent formative ideas are not directly perceived by the senses, but are intuited, comprehended, and acted upon *through* concrete experiencing. Plato held that learning itself is actually remembrance ... the *soul (holon) remembers**, including the informing dialectic polarities and patterns of sense experience descending from the Ideas. The holosophic formulation of the actual *Kosmic* pattern (or grid) *builds on that tradition,* and is intended through directive dialogue to restore gradual awareness of the primal Core of existence, i.e., "nature's DNA," and insightfully *remove* its trauma-associated, obstructing and *dis*abling *past mental-image* overlay.

The Buddhist idea of "alaya-vignana" or "stored *or basic* consciousness," like the more recent example of Jung's "collective unconscious," was based on the consideration that there was some kind of super-sensible projective formativeness, or *archetypal order* at the source and core of human consciousness, that had both purpose and reifying capacity. It was this enabling source that conceived (Be), actualized (Do) and perceived (Have) all *imminently* generated cosmic eventuality, and *domain* game interactivity.

---

* In the same sense that Platonic "anamnesis" or guided remembrance of past incarnation, restored the innate but "forgotten" knowledge of the soul.

> *A central failure of "the mind as a computational system" theory is that computations, per se, are devoid of meaning. They are purely syntactic ... devoid of semantics ... meaning derives from agency.*
> - S. Kaufman, biologist

Consider also, the primal triadic grammatical primitives of *all* language, e.g., subject, verb, object, as a cyclical ordering: be, do, have—which suggests a common source or "deep structure" of an innate linguistic, archetypal pattern-logic (or meta-mapping) underlying the cognitive orderliness of grammar, as well as the related *event-cycles* of common experience. *If we add a "knowing" capacity as the fourth innate source* from which the more obvious *triads* of being, doing, and having *emerge*, we can expand and reconcile the ancient polemic duality of the triad (3) *vs.* the *quaternity* (4) as the fundamental existential archetypal order (three for the Cosmos, four for the *Kosmos)*; by adding domains (7th & 8th) from which *all* logical order itself, is seemingly derived.

Sample Kosmic-Logic Agendas:

Linguistic order:	Subject	→	Verb	→	Object
Existential order:	Person	→	Process	→	Product
Metaphysical order:	Epistemic	→	Telic	→	Ontic
Archetypal order:	BE	→	DO	→	HAVE

Benefiting from the insights afforded by these enduring wisdom traditions, a *Kosmic* dialectic might then be considered as a *creatively ordered* pattern and telic (purposeful) progressive integration of opposing *ideas reified* as existence; as a dynamic and cascading series of historical occurrences. The philosopher Hegel combined these seminal ideas of a progressive cosmic "*event*ualization" into a triadic formalism which attempted to logically extend and develop the ancient Heraclitan opposites to achieve a *new* dialectical-historical process or "synthesis," and to integrate what is "true" and valuable in a universal continuum of historically evolving and self-reconciling experiential polarities.

> *What evidence is now available supports the view that all human languages share deep-seated properties of organization and structure. These properties ... these linguistic universals ... can be plausibly assumed to be an innate mental endowment, rather than the result of learning.*
> - Noam Chomsky, linguistic philosopher

Unfortunately, neither the Hegelian dialectic nor its more modern variations (e.g., Marxism) have any place for, or emphasis on, an innate, event-*causing* and broadly determinant *holon individuality, or persona.* One that could be a central, and localized, *conscious agency necessary* to the unfolding dialectic design and order of things, additionally and most importantly, no insight into the dialectic as expressing a soul-encoded, even *consensually templated order* for a universal *game*; or existence itself, *as the Kosmic Game,* that the "Absolute" could be playing. A purposive and progressive recreation, an unfolding displaying both Its divine and *cosmic*ally *creative* "*Self*-realization."

Building on these seminal insights and others, both ancient and modern, Holosophy, over many years of research, has developed a working, modular, and logically templated Code—attempting to formulate the primal domain-categorical patterns, *and themes*, of Kosmic existence. To categorize anything is a daunting task, and is in essence, a creative act since all "things," including symbols, are defined by a context which in turn is itself *selected* ... and that selection itself must be based on an *innate* and *order*-based intuition. An *essence* that must also *pragmatically* endow the Kosmic Code categorizations, *then* utilize the elements within each domain to project the vast gaming panoply of the Kosmos.

The Domains are a postulated matrix of primal e*xistence-categories*. Observably, they comprise the distinct but inextricably related sectors or arenas containing the creative purposiveness of a *Kosmic Game*! The uniqueness of each domain is established by its own categorical meaning-integrity, *and* by the spectrum of *category-purpose* associated existences, or "items," within its perimeter. Each domain also contains, as *sub*-categories,

> *Ideas or cognitive forms are the informing and regulative principles of reason ... since they arrange and order the objects of knowledge, they project fundamental and categorical ideational grids within which, and from which, all experience is made manifest.*
> *- Holosophic precept*

the primary purpose category concept of every *other* domain, e.g.: "the first domain's fifth domain," or "the eight domain's sixth domain." This assists the purpose of the "host" domain through its resident *symbiote* items, or items which may share characteristics of more than one domain but are primarily contained within each single domain category. These items both comprise and postulate each domain and provide a linking and communication channel of meaning for interactive *playful exchange between* the domains.

Whether an item of existence is perceived as "belonging to" or *within* one domain or another, depends upon the holon's ability to identify and differentiate between, each domain; as well as between the range of the sub-category items *within* the domain. *Awareness* of (1) the existence of, (2) the context and source of, (3) the distinctions between, and (4) the relative importances of each domain's characteristic sub-items, are necessary and vital data for effective participative decision-making, action, and exchanges within the game matrix as a whole.

This 'LIFE GAME' is an agreed-upon *Kosmic interplay* in which each of its domains *exchange* form or significance with all the remaining domains, in a *benevolent creative display expressed by and through the perceiving character* of each Holon-player. This character is a self-actualized *lens* or cognitive "contour of limitation" formed to accommodate the ethical requirements of playerhood; i.e., a game requires a level playing field and optimum rules and rational *limiting* conditions for *player presence,* participation, and *optimized* game continuity.

Sub-rational minds are essentially the fixed and limiting post-traumatic imposition of *mentally pictured* mass, (event) with

You cannot step into the same river twice.
- Heraclitus

location and *survival repetitive* significance but are ultimately generated by the being itself. These sub-rational confusions disable and inhibit the analytical differentiation necessary for *inter*activity and judgment *between and within* the domains. This blurring of conceptual distinction *between* domains and the resulting *un*awareness of their full category-existence, symbiotic, and sub-item content, causes the perceived omission, displacement, or inversion of the *exchangeable* components within the affected domains. This greatly reduces their *use*fulness as accurately identified items for the *rational and accurate exchange* of domain content to produce the greatest *gaming* good involving the greater number of domains; distorting perception of incremental betterment.

Post-traumatic false belief, pictured pain-associated identities, and other confusions, across the domain spectrum, cause sub-rational blurring by suppressing the free awareness and intention necessary to creatively be, do, and have all domains, and therefore, to fully actualize and empower the analytical choices and *rational exchanges* relating to optimum survival, and with suppression of its natural and rational *value*-discernment and actualization in all LIFE GAME modes of participation and play.

Ethics is based on the transcendent self-imposed obligation to make these rational choices for optimal game-exchanges on all domains. Thus, ethical playing of the game consists of creative goals and challenging problem-solving to bring about *finite increments of betterment as* conditions of play. The Life Game as *Kosmic Display* is the aesthetic contemplation of qualities and experience resulting from the *optimizing* interplay, or rising scale[*] of specified value-exchanges across the domains.

---

[*]An *up* staircase of increasing qualitative distinction of item or circumstance.

A neural network (in attempting artificial intelligence) can't do logical r*easoning because ... it* calculates *probabilities, but can't understand what those numbers really* mean.
- Marvin Minsky, neuroscientist

Following are some definitive purpose-categories that distinguish each domain, and selected words representative of typical sub-items from its category, sub-categories and symbiotes, both *freely* analytical (rational) and "compulsive" (sub-rational). These category references may be amplified and used in various ways to accomplish dialoguing objectives and general case[*] advancement.

1. Increase client awareness of all inverted, displaced, or omitted domain category distinctions.

2. Enable the client to create (and avoid violating) the integrity of a domain and its rational components, and never omit it entirely from necessary ethical computational considerations.

3. To facilitate by drill the ability to recontextualize both "inter-" and "intra-domain" item definitions necessary to restore optimal item placement, with communication and exchange between domains.

4. To provide an advanced case-entry items[**] perspective for actions in various professional dialogue modalities that target erasures of primal false beliefs containing past identities and other traumatically injected sources of aberration.

5. To restore by dialogue the ability to fully contextualize any item to fit conceptually within any domain with any assignment of order or importance, at will; and, as required, to postulate and attain higher ethical purposes with optimally valued envisionings and productively (ideal scenes).

---

[*]This references the use of this volume in Holosophy counseling procedures where "case" signifies the targeted "case contour or sub-rational belief and memory repository" of the client. The goal being the total *erasure* of all sub-rational impediments to *full* use of consciousness and ability.

[**]Any specified and/or experiencable element or aspect of a domain.

> *There is a reason in nature why something should exist ... rather than not ... This is a final sufficient reason[+] for things called God ...*
> -G.F. Leibniz, philosopher

6. To provide the necessary higher awareness of *pan*-domain perspectives required for achieving more advanced optimizing discussions and awareness; i.e., further reduction of the sub-volitional projection of charged memorial images onto other domains by *focusing the restored erasing power of the first (persona)*.

The general objective is to end up with a "living" and truthfully paradigmatic instrumentality that can act as a guide to re-align and correct *any* sub-rational domain *misplacement* of the elements (items) of ordinary experience. This enables a more usefully accurate complementary integration with the "conceptual deep structure" of the ascendantly scaled categorical order of the Kosmic Domains.

A Kosmos that is viewed with "rational pragmatics," i.e., using *best efforts* to achieve *incremental* betterment on an *idealized* scale of *total* multi-domain integrated quality and value, but often "settling" *rationally*, for a practical "viability estimate" of possible betterment. An *achievable result* that is based on *real, but temporal* and game-*limited* human capacity ... *but* ideally excludes *no* domain, or ability level in making or exercising optimizing judgments.

[+] It is interesting to note that, historically, "sufficient reason" has sometimes been defined as meaning that *all* knowledge and experience is derived from, and/or limited by a casual framework (Leibniz) or sense perception (Hume) or that ultimately all is conceptually "unknowable" (Kant) or that all knowledge is merely an extension of the human Will, that excludes the possibility of any ultimate and necessary being or reality (Schopenhaurer). By contrast, Holosophy posits an epistemic extension of the limiting traditional definition of the "sufficient" boundaries of reason, and holds that reason is *not* cosmically or materially generated, as above. It is rather Kosmic in origin; and the authentic Self is a volitional non-material conduit for accessing *all* cognitive capacity. It also has the willful and knowing ability to selectively self-limit its awareness to accommodate and *generate* its co-experience of a cosmic Playground in which logic and sufficiency of reason are *consensually agreed to* but the higher Kosmic rules of play-potentiality are pre-immanent.

> *Platonic existence as I see it refers to the existence of an objective external* standard
> *that is not dependent on our individual opinions nor upon our particular culture.*
> \- Sir Roger Penrose, physicist

The following material contains instructional examples based on both Holosophic counseling experience, and consciousness research, including philosophical and contemplation-based source materials, variably referenced in earlier publications. The Kosmic Code, and the content of the Four Perspectives of Kosmic orientation are suggested as a general guide for dialoguing application and seminar discussion ...

A final cautionary reminder: *No* mere symbology however pragmatically useful or accurately referential, is itself *ultimately* Truthful*. *That* Truth lies in the *a priori* and *meta-cognitive knowingness* that all mere symbols reflect, *and are derived.* Access to the guiding Source behind *all* symbols**, is the goal of the contemplative use of transformative dialoguing, with its *sub*-rationality targeting "inference cascade," enabling restoration of the basic *holosophy* objective: an expanded and optimized *Kosmic* participation by all holons!

---

* Higher consciousness, as the *ultimate* background of all existence, must contain the transcendent order (*ultimate* sufficient reason?) which makes things manifest. That order must have within it hierarchic *levels* of truth. These innate epistemic principles form the basis of our enthralled consensual co-experiencing of the Kosmos. *Objective* values including ethics are based on the ultimate primacy of the formative agreements of all holons ... earlier agreements have precedence. "True and false, bad and good," are rationally and *choice-fully* committed graduated qualitative distinctions which holons objectively consult to discern and calculate optimization on the scale of ethical values and actions. Ultimate Truth is a *super*sensible ideal, which however, *projects* and rationally anchors relative truth, as *reified* experience, but, like Platonic Form, is not *itself* manifest *in the material world.*

**A further note on the "Golden Ratio" designation: The metaphysical elevation of a simple mathematical numeracy as a cognitive gateway to a fuller understanding of the beauty, harmony, and ultimate relevancy within the game of life seems, on its face, problematic. So it appears until we recognize that the mere physical implication of the word "mean" derives historically from a *non-*material source. That *supersensory* individual awareness itself, *endows* and cognitively *projects* all symbology *including mathematics*! It is appropriate therefore, to assign additional meaningful "golden" designation to include an innate symbol-*sourcing consciousness,* i.e., a holon *persona,* as well. The ratio itself is then elevated and given true *meta*physical distinction and a more rational inclusion, as a living *source* of mathematical signification within Holosophy's universal descriptive symbology.

Kosmic Domain Thematic Integrity:
I   Egosphere - self
II   Erosphere - sex/family
III Oligosphere - groups
IV   Anthroposphere - humankind
V   Biosphere - life forms
VI   Cosmosphere - physuical universe
XII Noosphere- conceptual reality
XIII Theosphere - infinite potential

Part I

EXPLORING the KOSMIC CODE:

Life Domain Category Themes
as the
Formative Archetypal
Order of the Kosmos

The word "reify" is used in Holosophy to mean the process of giving, non-material concepts substance and perceptual reality, i.e. ideas made flesh or given "local habitation and a name" as Shakespeare beautifully describes it.
- Holosophic definition

Kosmic Domain Perspectives I - IV

Perspective I
Domain Category Themes
(A Kosmic Meaning-Spectrum)

This first Kosmic perspective consists of a generally categorized sample of *items** within each domain's meaning-space; to help restore a basic empirical certainty that *Kosmic* existence *has* a primal archetypal pattern, and that fuller knowledge of its structure and constituent parts *has* in fact, practical and distinctive multi-domain application and optimizing values.

Definitive standards used in Perspective I for the rational *intra*-domain categories of understanding and *relevant domain placement* of any *Word, Reference*, or *Item* (W/R/I). These are defined as follows: *a Word* as a verbal or written symbol with a distinct or *specified* meaning, e.g., "*dogs* I've owned." *References* as words symbolizing, or *referring* to *general categories* of things, e.g., "canine animals," and *Items* as the directly referenced *particular things* of the category within the domain, e.g., "Fido."

Relevant Counseling Instructions and Queries:

1. Is the full *defined* or multiple meaning of the general item–relevant W/R/I understood?

---

*Selection of domain WRIs occur as part of a Holosophic counseling procedure which attempts to help client to fully identify, accurately restore, and align rational domain meaning, placement, and perspective. Actually, *any* WRI is an item or existential *thing* in the general sense, for targeted address, in dialogue, so the above should have a somewhat permissive application!

The good is the intellect which comprehends what must be done ... and what must not *be done.*
- Bhagavad Gita

2. Is the full *context* of the W/R/I available, stated, relevant?

3. Does the W/R/I seem to have multi-domain item application? To which domain is it *mostly* applicable? Least applicable? Test the W/R/I applicability to other domains ... which domain's conceptual integrity best encompasses the W/R/I in a relevant decision-making and *optimizing* context?

4. Is there an interpretation or slant given to the W/R/I which exaggerates or diminishes its domain relevance as an applicable or optimizing factor?

5. If difficulty in domain distinction persists, apply *definitions*, *truth-functions**, and highest objective standards for its inclusion or omission as a relevant, representative item of *shared distinction*.

6. Always attribute meanings to W/R/Is that maximize and are consistent with their primary optimizing objective and agreed upon relevance and exchange-potential.

7. Does the placement or meaning you have designated for the W/R/I result in the *most* incremental *exchange* betterment when a practical choice is made? How does it contribute? How might its *absence*, diminished importance, or *wrong* meaning or placement be a detriment?

Each existential domain item (WRI) is subsumed in the category of broadest and most usefully distinct meaningfulness. *In this and the following domain perspectives, a few items were deliberately "misplaced" or mis-categorized to stimulate discussion and enable more precise categorical discernment.* Following are *examples* of the definitive *category* items or referent languaging that may

---

* See Appendix I for truth functions.

> *The brain doesn't produce thought, it filters it, to accommodate the experience of the ordinary.*
> *- Aldous Huxley, author*

accurately distinguish each domain (I through VIII) and their sub-categorically assistive, or symbiotic-items*.

I. **Holon** - individuality, one's own *persona*, consciousness, mind, character, self actualization, agency, identity, skills, ownership of bodily existence, characteristics, career identification, own body use, own mind use, own identity, earned personal decorations, awards, certificates, diplomas, viewpoints, urge to survive as individual or unique identity, capacity for choosing an interest or vocation, self improvement, study, motive for personal hygiene, self expression, recognition, continuity as player, personal certainty and endowment of participative intent.

II. **Procreativity** - family, product-food preparation, duplication, sperm, ovum, conception, childhood, mother, matriarch, patriarch, father, son, daughter, intercourse, home, desire, virility, muliebrity, impotence, marriage, seduction, infatuation, urge to procreate, sexual pleasure, sexual sensation, courting, contraceptives, homosexuality, bisexuality, sexual practice, rape, promiscuity, STD, relatives, family ties, incest, mother's milk, abortion, prenatal influence, mating, oestrus, nurturing, menstruation, sexual attraction, sibling rivalry.

III. **Community** - group, constituency, club, flag, insignia, meeting place, uniform, rank, the state, members, membership, law, rules, corporation, agreement, junta, team, team mates, constitution, politics, clique democracy, leaders,

---

* Each domain has reciprocal conceptual integrities and item distinctions of the other domains subordinately contained within it, permitting resonant *exchanges*. This enables potentially inter-applicable parts of the other domains as symbiotes, i.e., extra-domain *things* that (depending on proper attribution), contribute *exchange* value to a resident domain. This innate and contextual symbiotic capacity, is the basis of the *gaming* exchange between the domains; the primary dynamic nature of existence as *interex*changing Kosmic game *display* (see Perspective II).

> *In the beginning there was nothing ... and the Lord said "Let there be light" and there was still nothing ... but now you could see it.*
> *- T. Pratchett, physicist*

followers, morals, commandments, policy, administration, organization, orders, school, education, exchange, police, cadre, prison, criminal mores, language, urge to join, government, democracy, tyranny, aristocracy, collective.

IV. **Humanity** - human race, commerce, human species, ecology, world travel, space travel, exploration, brotherhood, united nations, world organization, world trade, confederations, world citizenship, league of nations, world treaties, fanaticism, international agreements, human rights, world systems, Esperanto, world health, world communication, hegemony, urge to act in concert as specie, free trade, global contract, world government, human dignity, common man's benefit.

V. **Biology** - life forms, plants, animals, primates, bodies, birds, vivisection, reptiles, fish, cell, virus, embryo, egg, organic form, seed, insect, mollusk, uchen, protozoa, organs, tissue, bloom, chlorophyll, protein, amino acids, RNA, DNA, genes, epigenetics, garden, harvest, pets, ecology, pollution, extraterrestrials, aliens, elan vital, life energy, fertilizer nutrients, agriculture, husbandry, photon converter, urge to survive as life form, bacteria, pharmacology, health care, eugenics, epigenetics, microcondria, ozone.

VI. **Cosmology** - physical universe, material, gravity, wave length, object, mass, atom, molecule, substance, smoke clouds, particle, fluids, chemicals, mineral, rock, earth, planet, star, plasma, air, galaxy, solar system, physical universe, shape, size, entanglement, elements, direction, vector, wave form, ridge, beam, explosion, implosion, orbits, black hole, rays, subatomic particles, quantum applications, electricity,

> *We cannot perceive full potentia (ψ) the common essence of things of the same kind ... an innate categorical potential for all associative meaning ... but only the observed forms of it that our conscious interactions create, thus our perception and awareness gives to possibility ... reality.*
> - Holosophic precept

    density, compounds, vacuum, mixtures, weather, wind, fire, water, location, tendency to persist, condense.

VII. **Conceptuality** - aesthetic wave, value, ghost, spirituality, art object, imaginal, beauty, the occult, magic, voodoo, mediums, masters, symmetry, book, sourcing-ness, logic, creative urge, sublimation, ambiguity, poetry, symbol, theory, idea, language, virtue, category, architecture, literature, abstraction, writing, imagination, mathematics, virtue, evil, courage, objective truth, goodness, purity, universals, astral body, ectoplasm, telepathy, telekinesis, metaphysics, ethics, justice, philosophy, immortality, freedom, free will, nobility, style, urge to create, effulgences.

VIII. **Infinity*** - deism, religion, worship, god, blessings, profanity, priest, guru, avatar, sacrifice, omnipotence, such-ness, omnipresence, grace, epiphany, transcendence, church, prayer, religious practice, rites, *infinite potential*, Absolute, theology, that-ness, basic truth, is-ness, hymn, miracles, divine healing, faith, belief, idols, sacred, infinity, unspecified knowingness, sacred texts, gospels, sutras, non-duality, parables, radiance, blasphemy, ultimate truth/self, pantheism, transcendence, sacred teachings, demon, heaven, hell, devil, angel, paradise, wrath of god, god-like states, idolatry.

---

*It is seemingly paradoxical to attempt to define something that is actually The Source of *all* definitions! This attempt, however, is based on the epistemic realization that the Deity is Omnipresent (on all domains) and therefore in a potentially transcendent sense, *un*limited in all *Its* aspects ...*including* describability!

That which is creative ... must create itself ...
- John Keats, Poet

Perspective I, contemplative exercises

1. Define and use in conversation some basic and preliminary terms of reference:

Categorize	Innate	Dialectic	Pronoun
Domain	Grid	Reify	Selective
Theme	Polysemous	Order	Placement

2. Do you perceive and understand the basic logic* and derivative eight domain order of the Kosmic Code? Does it meet the standards of the broader truth functions? Could it be improved? Discuss.

3. Select a few items from your ordinary experience and place them in the "proper" domain. Transpose a few items from one domain to another. Does any "thematic dissonance" occur? Why?

4. Do you understand the importance of mastering the "logic of domain categorization" and its importance to making rational choices and exchanges, as well as discerning relative importances? Explain.

5. Study the Kosmic formula in the appendix. Make sure you understand all of its distinctive elements. How does it apply to the interactive domain themes of the general Kosmic Code? Explain.

*Domains poorly recognized or identified cannnot be the object of rational choice for *inter domain exchange* which is, of course, the ultimate Kosmic *rationale for* integrative game exchange and its *domain display*. Pronoun language distribution for example, is used on domains 1-6 to specify particularity or plurality; a generic suffix is used on domains 7 and 8 to denote type and degrees of generality, materiality, and abstraction:

1	2-5	6	7,8
⏝	⏝	⏝	⏝
I, me	we, they	it, that one	ity, ness, ion

17

> *'There is no truth' is a preformative contradiction;*
> *an idea which refutes itself!*
> - Holosophic precept

Perspective II
Domain Category Theme Interaction
(Kosmic Game Exchange)

This perspective presents prime domain sub-categorization showing the interconnectivity of all domains. As a working certainty of the reality of the primal Kosmic grid or eightfold categorization of the apparently daunting complexity of existence is achieved, it becomes increasingly apparent that each domain contains reflexive aspects of every other domain, permitting ethical, resonant, interactive *exchanges* as consensual Life-Game purpose of benevolent and ascending *Kosmic value* display.

The Kosmos *is a game of inter and intra domain exchanges.* Each domain must contain reflexive meaning-access to *all* other domains to enable that exchange. *Failure to discern* the potential categorical resonance *between* domains will necessarily *prevent* proper recognition, and *reciprocal placement,* of sub-categorical elements within inter-acting domains to maintain the category-integrity *necessary* for rational, optimizing, playful exchanges.

This also prevents their inclusion for *holon-player* evaluation in any optimizing *action-*calculus of "greater good" across the *total* domain-matrix gaming perspective*. Their *dis*placement or omission results, basically, from aberrant belief, and behavior flawed post-traumatic "survival" calculations. Right meaning and placement is also dependent on factors such as level of personal awareness and ability to perceive and evaluate the contextual relevance necessary to make optimal domain distinctions and judgments.

---

*"Matrix"—that which, and from which, something originates, forms or develops: New World Dictionary, in Holosophy; where primary conceptual categories or templates establish meaning, or *order and form* the contextual basis for bringing something (e.g., the Kosmos) into existence.

Modern physics impresses us particularly with the truth of the old doctrine, which teaches that there are realities existing apart from our sense perceptions, and that there are problems and conflicts where these realities are of greater value for us than the richest treasures of the world of experience ...
— Max Planck, physicist

Following is a full listing of domains with relevant domain-related and/or interactive aspects:

8th Domain (Theology)
Infinite Potentiality
Undifferentiated Knowingness Enabling the Specified Known
"Neither the one nor the many"
(Non-dual meta-cognitive Ground)

Omniscience	Omnipotence	Omnipresence
V	V	V
(BE)	(DO)	(HAVE)

7th Domain Aspect:
The *concepts* or categoricalities of Theology, God, religion, Truth, holiness ... conceptual contemplation of the *non-dual*, ultimate ground, such-ness, the enabled communication between vastly extended individualities, deified consensus, primal thralldom, unconverged infinities, unmanifest and unlimited intention.

6th Domain Aspect:
Churches, cathedrals, altars, graven images or icons, crucifixes, temples, rosary beads, sacred tablets, relics, idolatry, holy water, converged infinities, as form, singularities (points of manifestation).

5th Domain Aspect:
Sacrificial animals, eucharistic wafers, consecrated wine, spiritual healing, body as sacred Temple and God's image.

Life can be pulled by goals just as surely as it can be pushed by drives ....
- Viktor Frankl, Holocaust Survivor and Neurologist

4th Domain Aspect:
A "chosen" people, or the "condemned" people, synods, world religion, proselytization, holocausts, crusades, missionary work, caste systems.

3rd Domain Aspect:
Congregations, denominations, religious orders ... apostates, clergy, heretic, priesthood, devotees.

2nd Domain Aspect:
"Brides of Christ," tantric practices (sexual spirituality), genital worship, karessa, orgasm *as* spiritual union, "sacred" sexuality.

1st Domain Aspect:
God "named," personified, such as Christ, or the Buddha, "holy-witnessing," *personal* mystical experience, "one with God."

7th Domain (Epistemology)
Specified Conceptuality and Categoricality
(Particularized Knowingness)
Bounded or "Subtractions from" Infinity to a manifest limit

Enabling Truth	Goodness	Beauty
Spirit	Creativity	Value
V	V	V
(BE)	(DO)	(HAVE)

8th Domain Aspect:
Angels, archangels, seraphim, cherubim, ghosts, devils, demiurge, holoarchy, *enabled* epistemology, unspecified singularity, theoretical physics, potential infinities.

The deeper layer (of the personal unconscious) is universal ... it has contents and modes of behavior which are more or less the same in all individuals.
- C.G. Jung, psychiatrist

6th Domain Aspect:
Telekinesis, mental-image, complex ideation made substance, reified manifestation, concepts combined as perception.

5th Domain Aspect:
Values of bodies, aesthetic of bodies, opinions or judgments about bodies, bodies as vehicles of player-hood.

4th Domain Aspect:
Spiritual brotherhood, infinitely enhancing playfulness, higher purposes, thralldom of Game, consensual objectivity.

3rd Domain Aspect:
Friendship, comity, brotherly love, camaraderie, compassion for one's fellows, agreement.

2nd Domain Aspect:
Eroticism, sexual quality and attractiveness, virility, muliebrity, dynasty, aristocracy, clannishness, genetic lineage.

1st Domain Aspect:
Individuality, uniqueness, personality, identity, self as accessing perspective, player.

*Why does the eye see a thing more clearly in dreams
than the imagination does when awake?**
- Leonardo Da Vinci

6th Domain (Cosmology)
The Manifestly possible Physical Universe
(Cosmic eventuation from quantum-collapse of wave-form)

Minus entropy	Singularities	Galaxy
Matter	Time & Energy	Cosmic Existence
V	V	V
(BE)	(DO)	(HAVE)

8th Domain Aspect:
Pantheism, physico-theology, god seen as all "Creation" or *as* the Universe, Nature or the Cosmos *as* Kosmos, animism.

7th Domain Aspect:
The conceptual *categories* of matter, energy, space and time, and all considerations about them, from their study (chemistry, physical science, astronomy), to their aesthetics (*beauty* of a sunset, grandeur of a mountain range), to their descriptive quantities and qualities (velocity of a windstorm, intervals of hours or moments, basic quantum non-locality, field dimensions), specified singularity as cosmic vanishing (or origin) point.

5th Domain Aspect:
The organization or manifestation of the universe as fundamentally "alive" in all of its material forms, such as galaxies and solar systems and their components, material origins of life, animism, "elan vital."

4th Domain Aspect:
The various "species" of the universe-as-forms, such as galaxies, star types and planets, or primitively, earth, wind, fire and water, or the table of chemical elements.

*Because that *primal imaginal conceptuality (seeing) playfully hidden,* creates *the world.*

"...A mental image is conceptuality made visible ... and palpable"
- Holosophy precept

3rd Domain Aspect:
The various patterns, collections, arrangements or interactions comprising the physical universe, affinities or attractors, such as solar systems, constellations, silver mines, crystal formations, molecular affinities, cloud formations, weather patterns.

2nd Domain Aspect:
The perpetuative actions or events of the physical universe, such as chemical reactions, polarity, stellar formation, attraction and repulsion, expansion and contraction, explosion and implosion, fission and fusion, "mother nature," "god the father."

1st Domain Aspect:
Any useful particularity or named entification of a universe constituent such as Saturn, the Rock of Gibraltar, my hammer, your shoe, a molecule, "observed" or quantified, particle or wave.

5th Domain (Biology)
All Life Forms, Energies, Functions

Specie Phyla	Life energies	Bodies, cells, bio-generation
Phylogeny, Ontogeny	Biophysics, Mitosis	Life Sustaining Elements
V	V	V
(BE)	(DO)	(HAVE)

8th Domain Aspect:
"Reverence for life," naturalism, the "living god," any philosophy or religion that worships life forms as deities; life as *sacredly valuable*.

Surely any omnipotent Deity worthy of the name must have the relatively modest capacity for the benevolent and playfully forgetful self-limitation ... deemed necessary to Kosmically enjoy Itselves.
- Holosophic conjecture

7th Domain Aspect:
"Vitalism," the concepts or general categories of living beings, consciousness or awareness, the urge to survive[*], survival of the fittest, intelligent design, evolution natural selection, instincts, the process of birth, life and death, of change, growth and development, plus all symbiotic considerations, values, ideas, and knowingness *about* life.

6th Domain Aspect:
Organic chemistry, universe as "alive," photographs, drawings, charts, books, models and physiochemical descriptions or representations (paintings, sculptures, jewelry, pottery) of plants or animals or other living things.

4th Domain Aspect:
Genuses, sub-genuses or species of animals, horticultural varieties of plants, entomology, viral, or bacterial types.

3rd Domain Aspect:
Aggregate life forms, forests, jungles, zoos, ranches, game preserves, reefs, parks, gardens, dens, packs, herds, schools, swarms, nests, colonies, thickets, copses, groves, orchards, crops.

2nd Domain Aspect:
Sperm, eggs, seeds, spores, mitosis, copulation, fertilization, pollination, diverse gender propagation.

---

[*] The holon as an immortal spiritual being can do nothing *but* "survive" ... not as a *particular* identity or persona, but as the first domain *source-potentiality* "or persona" of a vast lineage of consecutive player-personas, which can be reduced sub-rationally to the narrow existential parameter of the cumulative chain of identity-content of every mentally traumatic incident. Each with its "survival" fixed and forever (minus *erasure*) memorialized to *copy* the *actual pattern*!

Plenitude Thinking: 'Everything that can exist will exist' ... Yes, but only when the created consensual rules of a specified cosmos permit its unique and persisting manifest extraction from the total, unspecified, Kosmic Potentiality.
-Holosophy premise

1st Domain Aspect:
Any uniquely specified, named living entity, Lassie, Fido, the Redwood Forest, a particular protozoan.

4th Domain (Human Society)
World Congregated Totality of Mankind as Organized Aggregates

Planetary unification of holons	Internationally purposive action	Intended global effects
V	V	V
(BE)	(DO)	(HAVE)

8th Domain Aspect:
Spiritual communities, messianic salvation, living saints, the papacy, enlightened beings, God-like representations, aesthetes, humanitarians, philanthropists, sages, enlightened statesmen.

7th Domain Aspect:
Concepts of virtue, ethics, morality, earned rank, fitness, rational politics, social philosophy, ideal human behavior, human traditions and history, utopian ideals, anthropology, idealized sociology, the arts as ideal Global purpose, or idealized helping professions and modalities.

6th Domain Aspect:
Generic representations of human form, idealized likenesses of the human form as manifest through paintings, sculptures, photographs, films and monuments; the gathering or dwelling places of man, such as cities, homes, hospitals, offices, sports arenas, cultural halls, stores, museums and tombs; the material humanity-related creations of man, such as clothing, hardware, packaged goods and processed foods.

Repetition with awareness is transformative
-Holosophy precept

5th Domain Aspect:
The manifestation of the human species through bodies, such as male bodies, female bodies, androgynous bodies, and all sub-types of bodies as characterized by height, weight, shape, race, age and general biological entification.

3rd Domain Aspect:
Subgrouping capacity of larger populated totalities, the non-familial, non-religious groups and congregations of humankind, as exemplified through inter-national political parties, civic communities, corporations, labor unions, associations, universities.

2nd Domain Aspect:
Sexually-identified groups of people—heterosexuals, homosexuals, bisexuals, transsexuals, asexuals, the polyamorous and celibates—plus any gender-based global associations, communities or groups.

1st Domain Aspect:
Any particular or specified entity with global or broadly communal joining capacity, as above.

3rd Domain (Groups of Individuals)
Local sub-systems of the Entire Class of Humanity

Locally congregated holons	Local action in concert	Local shared productivity
V	V	V
(BE)	(DO)	(HAVE)

8th Domain Aspect:
Pantheons, god groups, theocracies, Valhalla, Elysian fields, Olympian.

The universe is the moving image of eternity.
- Plato

7th Domain Aspect:
Concepts of affinity, comity, association, purpose, goal, duty, task, destiny, cooperation, segregation, alienation, socialization, order, agreement, harmony, belongingness—and *all* considerations, opinions and ideas about them.

6th Domain Aspect:
Universities, research centers, think tanks, meeting places, club houses, institutes; membership cards, medals, trophies, certificates and diplomas, emblems, uniforms, badges.

5th Domain Aspect:
Groups as living things, the tendency of groups to populate themselves through memberships, staffs, boards, closed communities or adherents to rules, beliefs or policies, group survival.

4th Domain Aspect:
Global aspects of groups, various "species" of groups, such as professional organizations (American Medical Association), secret fellowships (Freemasons), university alumnae (Yale class of '79), public corporations (IBM), non-profit associations (American Cancer Society).

2nd Domain Aspect:
The various ways in which groups, reproduce or regenerate themselves, such as through membership drives, recruitment, solicitation, initiation, franchising, pyramid scheming, legation, also orgiastic activity, group sexuality.

1st Domain Aspect:
Conceptual integrity of a group and its specific symbiotic and associated elements, a particular member of a group, such as the Shriner Bill Smith or an Avon Sales Representative, employee, etc.

How is the water of the brain turned into the rich wine of consciousness?
- Colin McGinn, philosopher

2nd Domain (Intimate Bonds)
Family & Sexual Relations

Gender identity	Pro-creative activity	Pro-creative and family outcomes (progeny, security)
V	V	V
(BE)	(DO)	(HAVE)

8th Domain Aspect:
Sex deities, sex as act of worship, "the sanctity of marriage."

7th Domain Aspect:
Concepts such as commitment, vows, fidelity, loyalty, bonding, uniting, marriage, erotic love, family, parenthood, childhood and procreation, plus any ideas, considerations, opinions or beliefs on these topics such as fidelity, or "the joy of sex," plus the *study* of family or sexual dynamics.

6th Domain Aspect:
Physical representations of family or sexual activity, wedding rings, photographs of family members or lovers, marriage licenses; erotic films, books, magazines; items used to enhance or enable sexual acts, erotic art; items or substances used to invite or stimulate sexual bonding, such as provocative clothing, perfume, make-up, or adornments.

5th Domain Aspect:
Re-productiveness process, the tendency for intimately-connected people to erotically embody their relationships, optimum pro-creative functionality.

4th Domain Aspect:
Sexually oriented communes, proselytization, the extension of sexual and family relationships, husband and wife, married couple,

> *Rationally experienced and pretended unawareness is the essence of Thralldom*
> *... and as a game enabling requirement, is distinguishable from a mere lie.*
> - Holosophic Maxim

the global father-son or mother-daughter relationship, polygamy, polyandry.

3rd Domain Aspect:
The tendency for intimately-related people to gather in group settings, weddings, honeymoons, family outings, vacations, reunions.

1st Domain Aspect:
The identification of a particular individual through his or her familial or sexual ties, such as a family man, a good mother, a caregiver or other provider.

1st Domain (Self)
Holon: The Individualized Spiritual Being Character,
Its character as a Self-actualized Agency

Viewpoint	Intention	Event
Person	Process	Product
V	V	V
(BE)	(DO)	(HAVE)

8th Domain Aspect:
The *person* as an individuation of God, i.e., the soul as a *subtractive* manifestation, aspect, or endowed image of the Deity's infinite potentiality.

7th Domain Aspect:
The conceptualities of *specified* identity, personality, character, uniqueness, persistence, individuality, viewpoint, experience, perspective, personal ideation; the knowingness, consciousness and playfulness of the holon; personal creativeness.

Wordless or imageless (conceptual) knowing ... is the innate generating landscape of all actualized potential.
- Holosophic precept

6th Domain Aspect:
An individual's personal physical creations, insignia, accoutrement, such as his paintings, music or literature; his clothing and personal effects; his home and possessions.

5th Domain Aspect:
An individual's body and all its singular and distinguishing characteristics, such as its unique fingerprints, speech patterns, hair color, physique.

4th Domain Aspect:
The tendency of the individual to self-characterize itself through repeating personal choices, "higher calling" or tastes (a passion for golf, a commitment to vegetarianism, a career in architecture).

3rd Domain Aspect:
The tendency of the individual to gravitate toward certain group's activities or espouse a group standard or ethos.

2nd Domain Aspect:
Auto-eroticism, narcissism, authentic gender identity and expression.

Perspective II, contemplative exercises

1. Redefine terms adding the exchange context to each of the domain perspectives:

Game	Order	Conceptual
Exchange	Classify	Conceptual integrity
Zero-sum	Categorize	Hierarchy
Multi-sum	Aspect	Relative importance
Gradient	Holoarchy	Code/Grid/Matrix
Truth-function	Polysemous	Blurred distinction

> *If you torture numbers (or words) long enough, you can get them to confess to anything.*
> - Holosophic maxim

2. Does exchange actually require that each domain have a conceptual "aspect" of every other domain? Why?

3. Think of some examples that are not given in the written materials, e.g., an item that is considered a 3rd domain aspect of the 2nd ... improperly?

4. Is there a difference for example, between the 1st domain aspect of the eighth and the eight domain aspect of the 1st? Explain.

5. What are the implications of the 7th and 8th domains relative to ordinary household decision-making, or in corporate matters ... coal mining ... shark fishing, etc?

6. Explain from your own experience the distinction between the 7th and 8th domains ... 1st and 8th ... 6th and 8th ... 2nd and 8th? Give examples.

7. Give a *personal* definition of Ethics based on the material covered so far.

Perspective III
Kosmic Life Game:
Primary Themes Paradigm

Below is an itemized sub-categorization of items to display the primary order and its implicit logic-placement of *triadic* meaning *within* each thematic domain. This attempts to demonstrate the internal *horizontal* logical order informing each potential event-cycle of every

Case contour: A post-traumatic mimicry of the, actual persona or character by the sub-rational mind, formed cumulatively over time, and consisting of the totality of stored sub-volitional responses that constitute the false 'replicant' pattern of identities and perception, which the holon mistakenly endows and enacts as one's "self" (continued on next page)

domain as well as the holoarchic* *vertical* order of all domains as parts of the *Kosmic* plenitude.

1st Domain

Holon: actual self, persona, authentic character, Individual viewpoint, unique, originating agency, or self-actualized window ...

BE ...	><	... DO ...	><	... HAVE
identity/name		mind		memorialization
self actualization		mentation		substantive mental image
viewpoint		belief formation		perceptic
individuality		imaginal projection		belief system
integrity		enlistability		roles/rank
personality		intelligence		reputation/awards
agency		ambition		pride/confidence
psychology		capacity to do		capacity to have/use/be
capacity to be real		act to realize full ...		insignias of ...
capacity to be self		potential		achievement/solution
transform/realize		motivation		completion
discipline/initiative		application of		habit
personal ideology		knowledge or ability		skill/awareness
interest				goal achieved

2nd Domain

Family: care and rearing of children, procreation, sexuality, gender, related companionship and thematic expression.

BE ...	><	... DO ...	><	... HAVE
husband/father		contribute to support		household
wife/mother		consensually		family shelter
matriarch		impregnation/conception		sexual pleasure
patriarch		enriching family activity		educated children
family member		recreation		stable marriage

---

* Holoarchy: a vertical logical order of Sources, agents, values, conditions and/or events, arranged to give useful and referential meaning to a vertically grouped, or *laddered*, spectrum of holons.. The grouping is higher to lower in terms of *density* of *any projected manifestation,* descending from a transcendent *non*-material Source capacity (7th domain).

> (continued) *depending on the traumatic content of the event or circumstance... the word 'case' is used in a multiple connotation; historically; as in "case" study... also as the aggregate compilation of sub-rational 'issues' and compulsions which comprise the 'encased' (and displaced) holon's surrogate "self's" multiple past trauma-installed identities and behavior.*
> — Holosophic definition

bread winner	vacations	good family
lover	family economy/planning	relationship
conception	virility/muliebrity	assets
sexology	desire/nurture	consumption
tradition	birth	health

3rd Domain

Groups: friendship, community, team, cooperative, collective, county.

BE ...	><	... DO ...	><	... HAVE
company		work effort		compensation
partnership		cooperation		task accomplishment
friendship		caring		support
society		interaction		norms
bureaucracy		exchange		conquest
sociology		force		order
government		conflict		peace
community		exchange		victory
club		charitable acts		membership
hegemony		law enforcement		money
police		criminality		legality
military		fiscal policy		jurisprudence
		annexation		injustice
		warfare		laws
		policies		legal decisions
		clearing		members
				verdicts

4th Domain

Humanity: race, *globality*, civilization, imperial, planetary, national.

BE ...	><	... DO ...	><	... HAVE
humankind		social networking		multi national benefit
world government		interpol		treaties
human commonality		internet		civilized norms
race		health research		disease eradication

> *The descent or devolution of consciousness must take place before any ascent or evolution can take place.*
> - Sri Aurobindo, mystic

people	trade agreements	world reserve currency
empire	space exploration	racial/hate crimes
UNICEF	eugenics	epidemics
UN	colonization	esperanto
international law	empire-building	contact with space
IMF	slavery	space colonies
human rights		human specie survival
peace corp		charity
specie		space station
ETs		
olympics		

5th Domain

Life Forms: bodies, ecology, conservation, *biology*, zoology.

BE ... ><	... DO ... ><	... HAVE
biology	life energy (elan vital)	cells
physiology	cellular resonance	organs
life studies	bio-electricity	genes
genetics	metastasis	disease
ecology	mitosis	health
husbandry	evolution	RNA/DNA
ontogeny	growth	preservation
phylogeny	mutation	specie survival
bodies	circulation	
biosphere	brain	
	neurons	
	morphogenetic fields	

6th Domain

Cosmology: physical universe, material world, multiverse.

BE ... ><	... DO ... ><	... HAVE
universe/space	qubit	solid objects
physics	singularity	planets
secular	physical law	energy flows
reductionist	electrodynamics	machinery
atom/particle	travel	spaces
cosmos	motion	photoelectrons
planet/galaxy	gravity	photons & electrons
solid/liquid/gas	force	impact

> *The point of philosophy is to start with something so simple as to not seem worth stating, and to end with something so paradoxical, no one will believe it.*
> — Bertrand Russell, philosopher

instrument	mine	measurement
process	process	things
wavelength	extract	elements
cosmogony	condense	activation
conception	stretch	
(BE) -> intention (epistemic)	(DO) -> implementative (telic)	(HAVE) -> condition/ result (ontic)

7th Domain

Specified conceptuality: innate, orderly, meaningfulness at the source of things manifest. Symbols are reified combined conceptual potentialities "poised" for useful manifestation as *intentional*, and projected, "closures" into event and "substance."

BE ... ><	... DO ... ><	... HAVE
noosphere	imaginality	concepts
imagination	dialoguing	combined conceptuality
conceivability	selective unawareness	gnosis cognition
imaginal capacity	agreeing	insight
prime thought	optimization/program	revelation
spiritual practitioner	contemplation	Kosmos
mentor	enthrall	realization
knowing	polemics	conceptuality
philosophy	opponency	portal
Sage/logician	reincarnation	patterns
abstraction	meditation	supramental archetypes
value/quality	Koan	order
prescience	grammar	language
certainty	optimizing	thralldom
paradoxicality	evaluating	consensus
incarnation		transformation

Habit is not to be flung out of the window, but to be coaxed downstairs a step at a time.
- Mark Twain

8th Domain

Infinite potential for enabling specified concepts, the ultimate ground of all potential knowing.

BE ...	><	... DO ...	><	... HAVE
gods		apotheoses		epiphany
the Absolute		prayer/worship		illumination
deities/demiurges		spiritual practice		nirvana
theology		integration		that-ness
clergy		blessing		shared knowing
celestial		miracle		Mystery
such-ness		knowingness		all-ness
mysticality		infinite potentiality		Kosmic display
godhead		eternity		(Divine recreational)
neither the one nor many		creative act		miracles
one without a second		panentheism		pure working
super-soul				
capacity for knowing				

Perspective III, Normalization Drill

1. Difference between *your* 1st domain and *the* 1st domain? Then apply to 2-8.

2. Difference between your 1st domain and *another's* 1st domain? Apply to 2-8.

3. Difference between your 1st domain and *all* 1st domains? Apply to 2-8.

4. Difference between *all* 1st domains and *the* 1st domain? Apply to 2-8.

5. What is a 1st domain *aspect* of 2nd domain? Apply to 2-8.

6. How do the domains exchange? Assign value to exchangeables?

7. Differences between a domain's basic conceptual integrity and apparent existential aspects. (Elements that are properly

How can a computer be given a list of relevant contents, when no one, certainly not the programmer, has any idea of the extent or nature of the list?
— D. Berlinski, mathematician

relevant to each domain)?

8. What does exchange *between* domains have to do with aspects *within* each domain?

9. Spot the Know>Source>Create>Cause/Effect hierarchy within each domain.

10. How does Sub-Rational mind effect domain integrity/ exchange (Mis-placement, mis-definition, omission)?

11. Spot and describe Holon on/in *wrong* domain.

12. Relocate any sub-rational indicators to correct domain.

13. Relocate any problem item of interest, or fixed attention, to correct domain.

14. Spot sub-rational indicators/domain displacement:

   Is your 1st domain falsely located on another domain?

   Is your 2nd domain?

   Domains poorly differentiated must be differentiated before they can be integrated in any rational Kosmic inter-domain exchange activity or optimization calculation; explain?

Sub-rational Domain Displacement Exercise:
(Sample advanced client executions with counselor-comments in parenthesis)

Difference between your 1st Domain and *the* 1st Domain? Apply 2-8.

1st Domain: Everything that is distinctly personal, one's individuality, basic personality and agency as distinct from

God is man ... purified.
- J. Krishnamurti

another's (or *all* others).

Character:
- What is put forth when participating in life game. My participation is unique to myself and creates distinct communication possibilities when interacting across other domains.
- Self projected as responsible for past, present, and future actions.
- Spontaneously outgoing, engaged in life, ethical.

Appearance:
- Clean cut, enjoy style and fashion.
- Like to win and look good in the process
- Physical attributes are advantageous, enjoy any endowed physical characteristics

Position/Perspective on the game:
- Prefer leadership role
- More vision driven than consensus driven
- Open to change if a better path is identified
- Unwanted conditions—denial/disabling of higher purpose in life, restrained power in certain situations, overly concerned with appearance, unnecessary self-criticism

Difference between my 1st Domain and the 1st Domain.

General categories of the 1st Domain become specified, identified and listed versus the vast potential of 1st Domain. This is the distinct uniqueness that is my 1st Domain. (Note: the *generic conceptual individuality*.)

Difference between your 2nd Domain and *the* 2nd Domain?

Family/Procreation
- More emphasis on selecting a mate – partnership,

Seek the emptiness prior to the symbol.
- Zen saying

    lover, friend, and mutual fan versus procreation
    Parents, Children, Sister/Brother, in-laws are valued and important but not to the exclusion of others
    Not a strong desire to create offspring

Difference between my 2nd Domain and the 2nd Domain.

If family and procreation are equality split for category, assumed for this example, my 2nd Domain is heavily weighted toward a loving partnership in the present versus creating a next generation.

Difference between your 3rd Domain and *the* 3rd Domain?

Group/Community

- Love my career and the individuals associated
- Leading, building and helping others to achieve an ideal outcome is my passion
- Provide leadership that is productive, measured and acknowledged
- Forge a win/win mentality in all relationships
- Association with other groups – Holosophy, politics, the arts

Difference between my 3rd Domain and the 3rd Domain.

My particular 3rd Domain is distinct from the broader totality of the 3rd, but contributes to it.

Difference between your 4th Domain and *the* 4th Domain?

Humanity

- Organizations I support – Doctors Without Borders, local Children's Hospital, and Cancer Society
- Try to conserve natural resources and avoid excess waste (wrong domain)
- Support and engage with individuals based on uniqueness and try to discriminate because of ethnicity or beliefs
- Act to benefit most people that I can – each day,

> *Mind has erected the objective outside world ... out of its own stuff.*
> \- Erwin Shroedinger, physicist

accomplish some betterment

Difference between my 4th Domain and the 4th Domain.

Align well, difference is my uniqueness.

Difference between your 5th Domain and *the* 5th Domain?
Biology

- Exercise regularly
- Maintain a balanced, healthy diet
- Conserve natural resources—shepherd planetary and biological resources (again, wrong domain, 5th vs. 6th)

Difference between my 5th Domain and the 5th Domain.

Difference between your 6th Domain and *the* 6th Domain?
Cosmology

Reflects the urge to manifest through the physical universe, expressed havingness:

- Objects/Places—Appreciate my possessions more and provide proper care and treatment
- Events—travel, concerts, plays, movies, music lectures
- Maintain healthy body to perform and optimize participation (again 5th vs. 6th)
- Energies/form—Creating (7th D) into a physical document or mass for communication, teaching, coaching and expanding—TAP, Quality Sales Call, Team Selling, Sales Trac, IOB for RVS Distributors, to mention a few

My 6th Domain haveables considered in context of broader category of 6th Domain as potential Kosmic playing field.

Difference between your 7th Domain and *the* 7th Domain?
Conceptuality actualized through specified conceptualities, creating manifest choice from infinite potential (no, from *specified*

Identity is a subjective sense of an invigorating sameness and continuity.
  - Eric Erikson, Psychiatrist

potential re 7th Domain).

- Creating across all D's has greatly expanded
- Ability to will/manifest specific futures
- Projected feeling, tasting, emotions unique to my persona (confusing 1st and 7th)
- Unwanted conditions—fixed gradients which inhibit rational creativity, when facing a challenge, which isn't or hasn't been confronted—intention isn't directed to my full benefit rather directed to RI—spot any RI that limit optimized conceptual application and creation.

My 7th Domain has been greatly expanded. As more increments of betterment are attained, further expansion across all Domains will be achieved. (Unclear should emphasize conceptual regulation as source, not authority.)

Difference between your 8th Domain and *the* 8th Domain?

Infinite potential, Supreme Being, Source of Sources. Contains the potential of all other domains to manifest without expressing itself as any one, or being itself completely defined or delineated as a conceptualized entity.

- Recognize the unlimited possibilities that the 8th Domain provides (should be infinite *potential*)
- No single association with any one God or religion—accepting of all ethical religions (acceptance with rational differentiation and discrimination)
- Open to higher spiritual insight—self as God, creating or destroying (8th domains 1st as infinite *potential* personification)

My 8th Domain is part of the 8th Domain. Know more is yet ahead and attainment will allow for the right engagement and action in the Kosmic Life game. (OK ... but the *potential* infinitude is a different and "higher" order of magnitude than a *realized* 1st domain.)

> *Familiarity is memorial* knowing, *not the supposed re-picturing of the past by "brain states."*
> -Holosophy Canon

Perspective IV
Introduction

Examination and enhancement of each personal domain aspect of the Life-Game Pattern: Here we undertake, an overall *optimizing* review and reassessment of how we are currently *choosing* to live our lives. As purposes are clarified and disabling belief systems and traumatic memorial impediments are discarded, we are charged anew as holon-players to revitalize and optimally re-*normalize* our personal Kosmic Ethos and Game-Plan:

For example, if 7th domain awareness has been previously obscured by false traumatic image imposition or distortion, we may now find ourselves with new appreciation of objective *standards of value* and find new impetus to emphasize qualitative distinctions* in calculating how we educate our children or elevate our standards for making social, aesthetic, and general *Kosmic optimization of life* decisions.

Personal Domain Enhancement
(Improvement Possibility Review)

Perspective IV Domain Assessment Drills

Recognition and Erasure of Sub-rational Impediments

- Domains that are working (properly identified and "*itemized*"
- Domains that need work (unwanted conditions)

---

*The Calculus of Optimization is the innate cognitive instrument of rational assignment of choices to be made for maximizing the greatest good across the domains with corresponding increase of survival and general qualitative enhancement of life.

Discouragement is the only illness.
-George Bernard Shaw, Playwright

- Domains that are getting no attention at all (no domain *awareness*)
- Domains that are not clearly defined or distinct as domains

Stable Datum: Consult each domain for expanded exchanges that can be made/exploited. Is anything misplaced? Undefined? Resisted? Not valued?

1st Domain

- Realizing possibility enhanced abilities?
- Removing obstacles, unwanted condition, omitted purpose, Success Reluctance indicators?
- Upgrading self-worth and the ability enhancement that goes along with personal certitude and actualization.
- Increased *self*-awareness will create expansive awareness of, and creative interest in, *all* domains

2nd Domain

- Enhancements to 2nd domain relationships
    - Ideal of self-improvement as intimate partner, caregiver
    - Quality of life—externally, i.e., house, aesthetics, art
    - Expanding family recreational aspects and mutually enjoyed projects and activities
    - Expand intellectual family member interactions, with honest, productive communication
- Consider qualitative activity from other domains that can enhance relationships, family projects, vacations, home study, etc.

3rd Domain

- Increased competence as a manager/employee/team member?
- Larger zone of responsibility?

> *The ultimate nature of a Supreme Deity lies in the transcendent epistemic background which enables mere gods to communicate and collaborate.*
> — G. Greenstein, physicist

- Defining/refining ideas of team process and productivity = results in increased enjoyment of work product
- Deeper understanding groups and elements of 3rd domain, i.e., what is optimum human interaction at this level?
- Improve compensation/earning capacity
- Long term security goals defined and planned
- Upgrading ethical group contribution to other domains, greater knowledge and application of optimization calculus.

4th Domain

- Broader awareness of planetary and global issues affecting all people
- Broader world affairs knowledgeability
- Sense of being able to better influence/participate on world stage
- Introduction of global ideals—e.g., world peace
- Refinement of world government to better recognize and encourage individual awareness of *real* planetary issues.
- Valuation, acknowledgment, and enhancement of relations between heritages and between races without blurring the distinctions.
- Higher ideals
    - Value of individual over government
    - Free Market/exchange
    - No welfare/victimization/entitlement ideals
- International dynamics of world affairs
- Deeper understanding of how these things influence 3rd domain
- Ethical interaction
    - Rational, optimizing choices (global betterment)
    - Attaining higher ideals—aspiring to greater (objective) planetary good

What is the Universe? Is it a cosmic joke, a giant computer, a work of art by a Supreme Being, or simply an experiment?
- Heinz Pagels, physicist

5th Domain

- What is the "real" truth of global warming? Is it politicized?
- Wider view of life origins, life energy, care of the body, health
- Application of higher health norms, and information to self and others
- General life-sciences research expansion
- Disease prevention
- Research of disease, and palliative effects of spiritual awareness on disease

6th Domain

- Lesser dependence on fossil fuels, but not at the abrupt expense of the broader economy
- Optimal use of natural resources
    - Fossil fuels
    - Gold and all precious metals
    - Water and Soil
    - Marble, granite and minerals
- Conservation/rational use and reuse of *all* products of the earth including:awarene   - Atmospheric/geo-thermal
    - Ocean resources
- Appreciation of quality and beauty of physical universe as playing field
- The science and exploration of cosmology and physical universe—chemistry/physics
- Studies of weather application and control
- Physical services to other domains that facilitate and enhance human existence, e.g., natural energy resources, solar, wind, etc.
- Space travel—exploration and habitation of cosmos at large

7th Domain

Something is alive only to the degree that it contains a contradiction [paradox] within it.
  - G. W. F. Hegel, philosopher

- Conceptual integrities and distinctions of all domains, maintained for rational application and utilization of Kosmic game exchanges
- Exploration of higher cognitive realms, i.e., aesthetics, value, along with focus on *source* of those manifest qualities
- Consider greater interactive enhancement context with other domains
- Celebration & exploration of ethics, rational choices, optimization calculus for qualitative benefits to all domains
- Optimize heightened value preferences, ideal goal scenarios for all domains
- Fostering and support of planetary cognitive optimization and dialogue
- Individual holons who are disincarnate—prior to a participative embodiment
- Understanding of optimized continuity of consciousness of spiritual participants, as part of recurrent Kosmic Game Cycles.
- Appreciation of the beauty and deeper meaning of the Life Game as a benevolent Kosmic Display

8th Domain
- Observance and celebration of an ideal of a supreme being as a Kosmos endowing, Infinite Potentiality (for *all* domain manifestation)
- Increased tolerance of others' spiritual beliefs as variable increments of Truth
- Recognized obligation to upgrade one's awareness of, and contact with, all supersensible existence
- Perennial philosophy that all religions hold in common but with focus on a general and *rationally* elevating Kosmic/perspective
- Contemplate the ultimate "why-ness" of things; Kosmos as volitional Holon game-display
- Consider anew the meanings of Infinite Potentiality and non-

> *The "Isness" (Istigeit) of which Meister Eckhart had spoken ... the Being of Plato—a transience that was yet eternal life; a perpetual perishing that was at the same time pure Being; a bundle of minute, unique particulars in which by some unspeakable and yet self-evident paradox, was to be seen ... the divine source of all existence."*
> — Aldous Huxley, essayist/novelist

duality, and their specified conceptual applicability to *all* domains

Kosmic Code Domain Optimization

Code Optimization Guidelines: Some basic principles of positive Code normalization by increments of applied judgment and action"

- This *optimization calculus* considers, evaluates, and integrates perspectives of context, relative importance or placement distinction, both *intra-* and *inter-*domain, for the *greater good of the domains,* overall.

- Both sub-rational and natural limitation of character and ability can influence or modify *local choosing capacity*, but does not change or limit the innate and *broader* objective *Kosmic standards* for optimization and value.

- Proper domain placement of items is designed to reveal redundant and *mis*placed meaning categorization and enables its erasure (corrective *cessation* of creation and creative *re*-placement).

- Optimization is rationally choosing an action or inaction that *produces* the maximum *good*, or quality of rational survivability and existence for the maximum number of domains, i.e., objective *value* intuition or discernment that enacts broadly incremental game enhancement, i.e., optimized instances of progressive Kosmic thralldom[*].

---

[*]*Entrance*ment is sub-volitionally *pictured* (copied) thralldom ... goodness or true benevolence is rationally *enacted* thralldom ... "evil" is *that* natural goodness enforced and distorted by trance ... into a sub-rationally harmful and compulsive repetition ... imposing decisions and perceptions made and recorded under extreme duress, and later "applied" to "solve" that *false* stress-born confusion. Both neurotic and psychosomatic symptoms are apparently disabling replays of traumatic experience, *used* sub-rationally, to re-*solve* a challenging life-situation. Illness and disability are ultimate *"problem solutions"* mistakenly and redundantly self-imposed by the Holon to enforce a false ethical and "harmless" Kosmic participancy.

> *Geometry deals with ideal circles and triangles ... no real circles are exactly circular, no real triangles exactly triangular. It follows logically, that in general, all exact reasoning applies to ideas, not real things.*
> \- Lothar Schafer, physicist

- General concepts can have multi-domain framing relevance,
    e.g., perception   value   selectivity   ideal
          knowing   educate   game   abstract
          purpose   create   betterment   rational
    But each has optimum domain situational relevance when *made* meaningful within a specific optimizing context.

- Descriptions are not derivable from *earlier* descriptions, i.e., are not narrowly algorithmic ... it is the *knowingness underlying* the *convention* of verbal or symbolic languaging, unencumbered by sub-rational influence, that is the objective of dialoguing.

- The goal is to "think *conceptually* (without a *persisting mental image,* form, or referent) which instantiates and reifies *knowing** and familiarity (not memory) vital to making rational choices, i.e., *eventuates incremental* betterment (ethical optimization).

- The primal *anchoring basic* on all domain confusion is the first (earliest available) trauma-based deception, mis-definition, and resultant existential domain item *mis*-placements.

- Character is the *person*alized capacity for on-going creative assignment of domain distinctive meaning, choice, and control. All referents have determinant relevance within that specific meaning-space, and all chosen acts result *from and within it.*

- All sub-rationality and aberration has to do with traumatically distorted and *mis*placed domain-theme or item relevancy. Proper *re*-definition of domain, or *re*-placement of its item or word, reveals, and confirms the innate and optimizing knowingness that projects and imposes the actual Kosmic Pattern of Existence.

---

* Reification is the creative process of giving form and substance to *knowing* through *combined meanings* or concepts, e.g., length, breadth, width, solidity, color, form, more, less etc.

The world was made with time ... not in time.
- St. Augustine

- Imaginal or *conceptual* thought has contextual relevance but is also itself *distinctly* meaningful, and is *not* merely associative or algorithmically "programmed," as recovered *memory*.
- If a potentially *exchangeable* item is given wrong significance or domain placement, obviously its rational exchange-ability *is prevented*, since it "disappears" from its *actual exchangeable* location, and loses its proper *domain-relevant* designation.
- Rational choice (optimization) depends on correct assignment of proper domain-reference, itemization and importance. Any rationally chosen exchange implementation is a Kosmic *valuable-final-product* of optimized gaming interaction and depends on correct domain-identity and referencing:

(perception/analysis of value → rational *optimization* selection → actualized *valuable final* product)

- Exchange involves implicit exchangeable *opposition-potential* of all domain items, i.e., plus-minus, presence-absence, etc., exchange requires rationally opposed separation, as in dance, and *all* effective mutual interactivity.
- Use principle of maximum relevance to guide dialogues and *reduce* situational and interpretive variability. There is *always a transformative realization* when properly correcting an item's mis-placement or mis-definition. Obtaining each individual's real "best effort," although limited, is adequate when making rational choices. The goal of using this modality is to expand awareness and ability so that *better* choices and valuable *final* productivity are consistently made.
- Kosmic Code re-normalization must, *and does*, integrate many apparent philosophical (and paradoxical) conflicts*. Since numerous situational, contextual, or conceptual problems are resolved and integrated when the Holon's *personal, optimum*

*See Appendix I for further discussion and clarification.

> *Categories are pure concepts ... e.g., of unity, reality, causality, existence. They are forms that make understanding possible but are not part of the content of knowledge ... they arrange and order the object's nature, and make nature possible.*
> *- Immanuel Kant, philosopher*

attribution of domain placement and meaning, however traumatically distorted or *dis*placed, is revealed and usefully normalized (rational, location, function, and attribution is restored) through dialogue and erasure of post-traumatic belief and behavior.

Part II

Causation & Responsibility

with an Analysis of
The Blaming Mechanism and a
Representative List of
Contra-Survival Acts by Domain

All things truly wicked start from an innocence.
- Ernest Hemingway, author

Varieties of Causation

The representative categories of harmful or contra-survival actions and inactions referred to are not "sins" or "errors" in the traditional sense. However, *any* past *harmful* act or omission must be ultimately confrontable, *and have complete personal accountability,* if it is to be actually and fully acknowledged as *done* by the individual. The resulting erasure, insight, and re-assumption of personal responsibility removes *any* remembered past act as an obstacle to rational choice … since with post-erasure insight, the holon (person) can now *rationally create* or *not* create that act *in the present* … and doesn't *have* to post-traumatically *re*-create it as a *sub*-rationally generated *harmful* mental and/or *physical re*-enactment to again "survive" its occurrence! (See Part IV.)

What is a harmful act?

An intentional "contra-survival" act that doesn't contribute to the *greater good of the greatest number of domains of the Kosmos...*

It is any act that, in degrees, destroys, diminishes, debases, or demeans, *any* quality of life *not* for the greater good. An unethical act is one of sub-optimizing or harmful *sub*-rational *choice*, and is volitional by definition, since it is observable that a free choice *precedes and enables,* all sub-rational experiencing of existence. Such acts can be ones of:

Commission or Omission
(An Action or Inaction, and either Concealed or Acknowledged)

What is a "concealment"? A *tense hidden-ness* of an act (or inaction) considered discreditable or harmful:

We praise a man who feels angry on the right grounds, and against the right persons, and also in the right manner, at the right moment, and for the right length of time.
- Aristotle, philosopher

1. A sub-rationally secret or hidden point of view; or hidden and *enforced* unwillingness to communicate, contact, admit, or participate.

2. A sub-rationally enforced need to *not* communicate a discreditable act, or a sub-rational resistance to disclosure of discreditable acts or omissions seen as "contra-survival" or harmful, when considering the maximum number of domains affected.

Simple examples:
- Exploitation
- Forcing/inhibiting (personal or associative) with harmful intent
- Failure to be *able* to reveal, or communicate *anything* discreditable. (Even *irrational* neutrality *can be* harmful.)
- *Not* acting for greater good, i.e., based on a disproportionate mis-evaluation, or distorted by imposing a false, post-traumatically *weighted* scale of "survival" value.
- Actions taken, that are inappropriate, i.e., based on *any* false fixed (post-traumatic) ideas, beliefs, or assumptions.

When an action *or* inaction doesn't contribute to *some* greater good, i.e., an incrementally enhanced quality of life across the domains, it is basically, and by prior *Kosmic*; standards and *agreements,* considered to be gradiently injurious and *ethically* subject to *rational restraint*. Blame[*], however, as *sub*-rational accusative targeting *is always* harmful...

[*]Blame is sub-rational *assignment* of *causal opponency* to another, or an external condition, with denial of any related personal causation or responsibility and accompanied by mal-emotion, destructive impulse, and *sub*-rational re-enactment as "victim" or "villain."

Numbers alone do not reveal the meaning of numbers ... numbers are not aware of, nor do they "understand" other numbers.
- Holosophic maxim

Corollary: The Blaming Mechanism
(Overt and Covert)

False and *mal*-emotionally judgmental *distortion* of this natural restraint, or censorious assignment of causation, i.e., blaming is the *primary* marker, symptom, or "flag" of often covert but always unethical, harming by the blamer *or* blaming *victim* ... all sub-rationality is, and requires, blame or primal mal-emotional assignment of cause.

Definition:
1. The Holon's compulsive mis-assignment of "game-opponency" to another, or an event, with *sub-volitional indicators*, and *mal-emotion*. It contains also the often hidden assumption of intentional harming by the "other" *and* with injured "innocence" on the part of the blamer/sufferer.
2. The Holon's hidden use of the sub-rational mind to create post-traumatic mental-emotional images in a *dis*-abling scenario that executes a sub-volitional purpose to be a victim, to "prove" one isn't a *villain* (success reluctance).
3. Another, *or* a circumstance, is assigned total responsibility for one's personal feelings, thoughts, problems, difficulties or condition! (*Omitted* awareness of primary individual *choice of response* to all events, as well as denied recognition of personal responsibility; tactical *mis*-perception, of *rational opposition as wrongful and harmful enmity*.)

> One must be able to admit *having caused* before one can refrain from causing.
> - Holosophic Precepts

Factors Preventing Blame Recognition

I. *Mis*-assignment of Causation:
- Failure to perceive actual source of that which *causes* or brings about a condition ... seeing another as the sole blamable cause of one's own actions, state, or volition ... a general mis-attribution of circumstances which actually *begin* a condition of existence or eventually ... convinced traumatic re-memorialization of painful effects, *displacing actual perception* of the immediate present and/or personal causation.

II. *Mal*-emotion
- Sub-volitional unawareness of mal-emotional feelings (boredom and below)* as direct indicators of blaming action. An instant sub-volitional re-definition of obvious and previously agreed to standards of blame recognition, in order to justify and continue a mal-emotional critique or angry targeting. *Mis*-perception of another as a bad, wrong or guilty, victimizer of self or others, often with tense denial of so doing.

III. *Mis*-ownership
- Denial of all awareness that one is ultimately responsible for one's condition, and is, at *a deeper* level, *contributing* to any unwanted condition or problematic situation experienced. One's actual continuing, and *volitional choice* to continue Kosmic participation, ultimately *endows* the primary sub-rationality of blame. All denial of the holon's full *volitional* participation in living, *sub*-rationally *substitutes blame for rational game-enabling opponency*!

---

*On a theoretical scale from pleasant, normative sentiment, descending by degree of response to perceived stress, from boredom down through levels of painfully conflicted (charged) emotional feelings; hostility, anger, and fear to final apathy and death.

There will always be mathematical statements seen to be true, that cannot be proven (or disproven) within one set of axioms. A "complete" set of axioms can never exist.
- Kurt Gödel, logician

Brief Self-Realization Drill (M→E→S→T)
*Categories used to identify,
evaluate, and erase sub-rational indicators*

I. **Mass** (sense of external solidity and contactability)
   - Accurate perception of mass and substance is without sub-rational distortion by superimposed post-traumatic imagery. These disabling mentally "pictured reminders" of the past impose a very poor *density discrimination* of the actual environment. The immediate present is *much* denser than the re-activated *mental images* from the past imposed *on the present* as a falsely projected "thereness." *Erasure* of this "misplaced concreteness" results in a sudden and revelatory *perception* of the previously sub-rationally displaced but now a very *real and present solidity* ... the *actual* Kosmos!

II. **Energy** (restored and appropriate emotional response)
   - Present awareness is often obscured by a triggered, enveloping, unpleasant feeling, or *mal*-emotion. This is *sub*-rational emotion is a "feeling-response" from the *traumatic past*, which inhibits rational response to present circumstances acting as a *compulsive* "reminding" mechanism. It floods the present with uncontrolled, *painful*-emotion "perceptions," which can inhibit current ethical discernment, and the capacity to make the rational choices necessary to be an effective Kosmic Player.

III. **Space** (awareness of looking through a distance *to* things)
   - Command of occupied spaces requires ability to discern and separate *out of* the seemingly "present" sub-rationally *pictured* spaces of the past. This restored spacial discernment re-enables—rational uses of actual spaces to execute the appropriate cycles of action necessary for

*You are not a human being having a spiritual experience,
you are a spiritual being having a human experience.*
- Teilhard de Chardin, Christian mystic

      optimizing productivity, i.e., the gaming exchange *inter-activity* between Kosmic domains.

IV. **Time** (cognitive re-familiarity vs. mental-image of past as "present")
- Essentially this requires the ability to distinguish and *control the location and flow* of memorial or imaginal temporal events free from all imposed and fixed *post-traumatic* memory.
- One must be able to differentiate space-times, and distinguish *past from present* to avoid compulsively *re*living a *past* traumatic experience; and to restore rational temporal goal sequencing, since optimizing game-enhancing causation, is always *motivated by the future (a goal, objective, or ideal)*!

Types of "Blame"
(Rationalizations for Sub-Rational Opponency for Review and Discussion)

I. Some examples of covert and disguised blaming:
- "My fault for letting them," "I was stupid enough to" (guilt implies blame of *something*)
- "If they cared, they would ..." "I'm disappointed" (insulated and un-admitted resentment)
- Unwilling, indefinite, or rationalized admission of *existing* resentment (*all* mal-emotion implies blame to some degree)
- A "perceived" *flaw* (when actually a *blamed* deficiency)
- Why me? Life is unfair and *essentially* blamable
- False synonym (Sub-optimum = bad, wrong ... focus = fixation ... limit = impairment ... delay = hesitation)

Perception in the presence of a sub-rational indicator is never accurate, nor ever the rational basis for any decision or action ... The world is always "green" when observed through a green lens ... rational actions require the "full-spectrum" data-input of Kosmic 'Technicolor' to guide our powers of choice.
- Holosophic precept

- But *they* really *(are)* (did) (have) the thing that is "wrong," "bad," (no awareness of sub-volitional "blame-framing" of the other)
- Always "poised for outrage" habitually resentful
- Entitled *resentfully* to "missing" or "denied" fair treatment, support or subsidy ... is "owed" what is desired or "needed"
- "Guilt" as disguised blame of the "other," e.g., blaming a false *pictured* "self" (case-contour) for a mistake or action
- Waiting ... blaming for delayed or absent stimulation of interest, not self-generated
- Being "subjected to," "deck stacked against me"
- Implied wrongness or accusation (expected better, more, disappointed, hoped, etc.)
- Regretted actions are the *blamed existence of past* "bad" actions
- Martyrdom—"good or noble suffering" *valued* pain
- Resented description ... "sticks and stones" *do* hurt
- Critical, taking *mal*-emotional exception to a perceived sub-optimum situation, person or thing ... expecting perfection in *others* and blaming its *absence*
- Impatience or boredom ... blaming a person or event for not being "interesting" or being "boring"
- Generalized protest without rational *countering* to change
- Persisting but un-remediable indignation; "*un*forgiveness"
- Not being helped *properly* or "enough"
- "Honest" confusion ... weren't told ... or explained to ... or properly informed, as excuses for blaming

He who despises himself nevertheless esteems himself as a self-despiser.
- F. Nietzsche, philosopher

- Promoting hopelessness, succumbing, "having to give up," or *have* to "play ball," resentfully—with "the system"
- Holding on to a resentfully *pictured* (memorial) injury, "offensive" remark, event, person, or thing ...

II. Interpretive descriptions or "factoids"* selectively "spun" as "*blamable* facts" or as *rationales* for blaming:
- Something, someone is "unhelpful" or actual help is "really" not appropriate or what it "should" be ... "a wrongful absence of something desired that *is* blamable"
- Arguing (mis-emotional protest) with a supposed untruth or falsity as opposed to rational *countering*.
- Reasonable *blame* of others for *blaming* (me, others)
- "Forgiveness" as covert blame, "they can't help themselves," "shouldn't have expected them to" ... (devaluates holons as natively responsible beings)
- Some *external* bad cause, e.g., "poverty" is considered *wholly* responsible for one's persisting unwanted condition
- Unperceived, sub-rational standard or belief justifying an apparent *non*-ideal scene, e.g., "never get a break"
- Effects of undeserved harm persisting ... pictured injustice/betrayal nurtured and festering as victimizations
- "Injustice collection" ... previous harming by self, requiring retributive redress ..."seeking compensatory suffering"
- *Tense* denial ... or a silent *protest* of one's communication or "self" being mis-represented, convinced of "need to be right"

---

*A temporary attribution, assumption, or speculation that, through repetition, becomes accepted as a fact.

The rational mind exists to selectively and automatically limit premature and game-revelatory Kosmic knowing...
- Holosophic maxim

- Dishonest non-participation that selectively resists *inferences* that lead to insight ... full consciousness defensively *reduced* to being mere substance (as mental picture) or "brain" process (mechanical enactment without admitted volition)

III. "Rational" blame: Righteous Indignation: some things "*are* bad" ... grudge or lingering animus based on "real" (but *memorially* pictured) injustice, or to endlessly "punish" the guilty ... being a "just" agent or instrument of "karma" or "cosmic retribution" ... a false but continuing "righteous" enmity disapproval or activity.

IV. The sub-voluntary mind itself is essentially the *primary* blaming mechanism since it *critically* asserts false values and basically projects and *enacts* false opponency using *disabling*, self-replacing *past* identities, and beliefs. *Past* traumatic scenarios are imposed on the *real pre*sent, hence, implicitly de-valuing and blaming their *picture* for past "harmful causation"!

- Blame empowers opposition, falsely ... creates "enemies" not opponents, and justifies *enacting* all sub-rationality as hidden "evil" purpose to destroy "threats to survival"
- Blame disables rational choice and influence
- Blame makes being helped difficult/impossible
- Blame discourages contribution, compliance and commitment to any rational common effort
- Blame constructs and feeds the illusion of "uncaused" innocent and continual suffering or victimization ... which must then be covertly fought and "avenged" ... (retributive reflex)

That which lays at the root of each of us lays at the root of the Cosmos too.
  - F.W.H. Myers, philosopher

- Blame *energizes* tension-based psycho-somatic illness
- Blame enacts a rationalized punitive isolation of self from others as harmers ... "menacers"
- Blame is corrosive, both physically and mentally ... it prevents the *erasure* (with forgiveness as a resulting and *freeing access to novelty*) needed to draw *rational* inferences from past experiences, release tension, and initiate right action in the present
- Blame is also misplaced and distorted (but selective) perception leading to a retributive cycle of *receiving compensatory* harmful acts, or omissions, affecting self

V. A blaming tendency is remedied by the incremental restoration of the certainty of causation of *all* personal opponency and the confidence that one can confront and erase one's *primal identity-eclipsing* traumatic stress. Doing so removes all resultant victim behavior, by restoring ownership and resulting erasure of any compulsive mental *picturing* with its *sub*-volitional displacement of all authentic selfhood.

VI. Blame* is often covertly expressed as demanded compensatory "entitlement" or deserved remedy for victimizing deprivation:
  - No one is *entitled* to a gift ... real entitlement is discretionary and is based on rational contexts, agreements, and exchange of value ... not protest of denied expectation.

---

*Blame is *the* primal sub-rationally copied gaming impulse to oppose. It is the holon's basic sub-cognitive attitude toward the actual pattern of existence "*needing*" to be copied and "preserved," during an apparent (but mistaken) erasure by an injected false revelation during *extreme* duress. Blame is the *primal* mal-emotional mode of re-action by the holon, when under duress and "solving" a *false* revelatory threat to the game-in-progress by *obsessive opponency*...

> *There is no evil committed, even for its "own sake," or for no reason, that is not selected, therefore, preferred, therefore valued, and that consequently, must be referencing a scale of value which contains and implies a range and extension of some higher acknowledged Good.*
> — Holosophic canon

- Cognitive-optimization assumes innate and original participative willingness or casual capacity on part of any "blamer" or villain.
- Real charity is compassionate and not merely sympathetic.
- A *rational* request for and acceptance of assistance is never based on a resentful "neediness."
- To "need" rationally is actually to *require,* causatively without oppressive mal-emotion, or victimized perspective.
- What one *needs* to *assert* … one is never quite sure that one natively possesses or honestly controls.
- No limiting decision made or line drawn; should be for "eternity" … all *cosmic* "boundaries of belief," are set as *living* perimeters subject to *ultimate* rational change.

Kosmic Causation & Responsibility
(Sub-rational Departures From the Ideal by Domain)

Some examples of apparently evil* *intentional harming,* (irrational choices) by action, or in-action *considered by domain* and which upon careful review and contemplation may suggest some optimizing and *consensually objective* standards for human awareness, decision, and behavior; intended, when in evidence, as potential subjects for transformative dialogue:

---

*Holosophy defines "Evil" as 1. The quality of an *intentional* sub-optimum action or in-action resulting from choices made with forcibly sub-rational, *but covertly volitional*, elimination or distortion of present perception and value; *supplanting* the actual character decision, and action of the holon with the "case-contour" (sub-rational re-imposition of past identities, beliefs, decisions, data and enforced opponency); 2. Action, or in-action not for the *greater* good; which then distorts and diminishes any rational choice of betterment or optimization to serve a personal sub-rationally distorted intent or "good" solely based on a fixed *past* survivability. Actual goodness has prime priority over "evil" since any such evil act is seen by the perpetrator, when committed, as somehow sub-rationally *justified,* therefore *valued*, overtly or covertly as an intent, and therefore *a preferred* "good," see quote above.

> *Experiments have shown that the 'placebo belief effect' can make drugs that normally induce nausea settle an upset stomach ... and melt warts, cure seasickness, make sugarless saccharin raise blood glucose levels, relax bronchial spasms, neutralize poison ivy, and make normally harmless leaves poisonous.*
> \- Holosophic research archive

I. 1st Domain: Self/Casual Agency
   - Neglecting or invalidating opportunities to improve one's condition or status.
   - Lying/dishonesty/self-deception.
   - Knowing mis-representations.
   - Self-effacing, self-abnegation or obsessive valuation of others viewpoints over one's own.
   - Self-aggrandizing—"Must" be noticed, reassured, admired, obeyed.
   - Reducing awareness to accommodate a sub-optimal scenario ... "dumbing down."
   - Taking drugs to reduce or artificially stimulate personal "awareness" or sensation.
   - Failure to honestly observe, and communicate with, situations that should be handled; neglect of betterment increments.
   - Denying accountability as a self-determined *"agent"* of influence, or as having primary volition.
   - Imposing false, and actual-*self* displacing *other* domain elements.
   - Identification of intentions or concepts with "conditions."
   - Avoid confronting, or "backing off" from rational commitment, or the fulfilling of personal obligations or compliances.
   - Denial or disabling of one's true mission or higher purpose in life.

The spiritual factor in health is the critical factor in all healing. Illness is a derivative from the truth presented in a biological and emotional form or display of the false belief system we fear. The experiential world is the effect of our beliefs not the cause.
- Gerald Epstein MD, psychiatrist

- Sub-rational rejection, or unawareness of, one's primordial commitment to norms and objective standards of value, inherent in the consensual construction of the Life Game.
- Toleration or re-use of sub-rational indicators without remedial transformative effort, intent, or interest.
- Failure to perceive guilt or self-reprehension as a *sub-rational* indicator.
- Seeking degradation or self-abasement to assuage unconfronted sub-rational impulse, action, or memory.

II. 2nd Domain: Family/Procreation
- Neglected general welfare of one's family, failure to support progeny or plan and implement their future betterment.
- Failure to support/contribute/optimize—with regard to a family member, condition or situation … absence of reasonable "caring."
- Overtly injuring a family member, e.g., spousal abuse, etc.
- Infidelity, i.e., violation of rational vows.
- Discreditable sexual acts/sexual behavior that violates rationally agreed upon mores … or ethical community standards, e.g., seduction of minors—predator activity … behavior injurious to another aspect of the domain.
- Pedophilia
- Prostitution and procuring
- Rape
- Incest
- Dishonest providing of sexual services for reasons *other than* mutual enjoyment and fulfillment. (Optimal sex: no

> *In 'blindsight' researches, subjects with lesions in the visual cortex of the brain are still able to make accurate 'guesses' about the color and form of objects they are not able to 'consciously' see; a seeming capacity for consciousness of, without perceptual awareness of.*
> \- Holosophic research archive

Sub-rational Indicators, not injurious, mutually pleasurable, consensual, free, spontaneous, deeply satisfying.)

- Resistance to deepen, renew and expand the sustaining erotic value context of a committed relationship.
- Sexual compulsion/prohibition/addiction/obsessive or gratuitous seduction.
- Promiscuity which denies or obscures the values of exclusivity or the *multi*-domain implication of a sexual act.
- Failure to properly educate juveniles, transformatively.
- Abortion—if casually or superficially permissive, or devalued as exclusively on the 5th domain.
- Sexual intimidation/threats/stalking, or conversely disabled commitment capacity.
- Male or Female sub-rational domination or submissiveness.
- Acts which debase, demoralize or diminish the *person*-hood of a sexual partner.
- Calculated neglect or dismissal of any higher purpose or potentiality of sexual activity.
- Misuse of gender assumption that negates procreation, family, or care of children.
- Narrow and critical intolerance of another's sexual preferences, or forcefully imposing such standards.
- Any use of drugs or artificial stimulation which substitutes dependence or addiction for natural sexual ability or motivation.

> *The source and content of a memory, or any mental image, must already be known ... before it can be found and selected to appear as a representational image of a thing or event.*
> *- Holosophy maxim*

III. 3rd Domain: Group, Team, Cooperative Effort
- Betraying a team or group to whom you owe rational allegiance
- Failure to contribute best efforts to an assigned task, project, or program.
- Substandard productivity—not really producing what you have agreed to produce. Valueless products, unfinished, dishonest, wrong, or flawed products.
- Covertly "working against" those in authority without honest expressions of any grievance.
- Knowing violation of laws, rules or procedures known and agreed to be for a common good.
- Promoting and accepting unearned gratuities/compensation/bribes at the expense of one's group.
- Emphasizing "entitlement" over real productivity and compensatory exchange for valued contribution.
- Willful non-compliance after agreement to comply.
- Willful and disloyal counter-productivity.
- Espousing false or substitute goals and counter-purposes ahead of the rational goals of your own group.
- Leading group members astray by gossip, innuendo or *persistent* complaints through improper channels.
- Consistently putting self above interests of the group in *all* matters (1st domain = 3rd domain).
- Failure to institute, support, or enforce rational policies or codes of behavior that ensure group survival.

God used beautiful mathematics in creating the world.
- Paul Dirac, physicist

- Unwilling to recognize or support any rational umpiring system established to ensure observance of the "rules of play."
- Maintaining a counter-productive attitude or purpose as a group member with no attempt at remedy.
- As a member, seeking irrational destruction/defeat of group that its other members are loyal to.
- Active support of a competing or inimical external group.
- Failure to care for and develop one's individual subordinates for the group benefit.
- Harmful and covert counter purpose or intent.
- Reducing standards of excellence for group productivity, or failure to rationally maintain or increase them.
- Not supporting or actively opposing powers you have agreed to depend on.
- Failure to master the essentials of one's job functions while pretending to fulfill it.
- Willful creation of a deleterious group-reliance through a pattern of unwarranted assistance.
- Not understanding or following the rational* ethics conditions for a group activity.
- Insensitive to the need for level "playing fields" in all interactive endeavors; *multi*-sum game awareness.

IV. 4th Domain: Species, Mankind - "The Planetary Perspective"
- Countering any *global* awareness that considers mankind as a whole.

---

*Ethics is: a rational choicefulness made for the greater good of the greatest number of domains ... Benevolent prioritization of display and action expressing an innate and freely accepted obligation to purposefully enhance the Kosmic Life Game.

The Libet experiments showed that cortical brain activity associated with body movement begins three hundred milliseconds before the movement is consciously decided upon supposedly demonstrating that the individual "does not consciously initiate" the
(continued on next page)

- Failure to seek consistent cooperation/equitable interaction between pro-survivally productive economic, national or political structures.
- Seeking to disadvantage/undermine national or ethnic participation in global or planetary matters.
- Failure to establish, maintain, or misuse of, freely elected national governing bodies.
- Failure to enter into, support or violation of, international treaties, agreements or accords designed for the common good.
- Failure to promote or institute rational trade or immigration policies on national level.
- Failure to provide an international perspective and option for national or private charitable or educational functions.
- Seeking tyrannical global domination or hegemony.
- Fomenting radicalized global terroristic activity that bypasses public norms or decision making; for sub-rational ends, the free democratic process.
- Fomenting revolution … Not in the *actual* service of the common good.
- Denigrating or diminishing any higher concept of planetary commonwealth or purpose.
- Failure to consider and promote a cooperative non-biased planetary perspective with regard to race and minorities.

V. 5th Domain: All Life Forms, The Body, Ecology
- Failure to cultivate and shepherd planetary biological resources.

> *(continued) action. But how does the brain "know" in advance how to "correlate" its associative micro-neuron activity directly with the subsequent macro-conscious volitional intent of the person?*
> *- Holosophy hard question*

- Failure to provide proper nutrition and exercise to a body or bodies one is responsible for maintaining.
- Failure to protect and guarantee the optimum survival of endangered species.
- Tolerating or promoting the harmful existence of a life form that threatens higher life forms (e.g., no effective disease control or irrational relocation of a species like pythons to Florida).
- Displacing *natural* curative measures and capacities with enforced and *fixed* allopathic (vs. effective alternative) methodology or prohibitive laws.
- Emphasizing mere survival of the body over higher purpose and personal spiritual integrity.
- Poor or no hygienic practices.
- Failure to conserve biologically based resources (animal/plant/marine stocks).
- Neglecting or failing to emphasize or act upon natural charitable impulses that constructively address hunger, and disease in less privileged portions of the globe.
- No high minded application of optimized biological principle relating to agricultural and horticultural endeavors.
- Drug abuse ... seeking recreational usage of addictive substances to artificially "enhance" consciousness or sensation.
- Toleration or promotion of substandard nutritional ingredients or sources in foodstuffs.
- Toleration or failure to address constructively; pollution, toxic waste, artificial fertilization, and any disease producing biological additives.

A Paradigm is the image of the souls guiding inheritance ... selected to play within.
- Holosophy tenet

- Misuse of the RNA/DNA/Genome structure in ways that would be genetically harmful to any valued species or life as a whole.
- Failure to direct and control natural evolutionary processes or potentials which, perfected or improved, would contribute to the general welfare.
- Failure to have reverence for life in all its broadly optimized perspectives.

VI. 6th Domain: Physical Universe
- No reasonable conservation of planetary physical resources.
- Creation of artificial needs for natural resources in any section of population.
- Creating artificial scarcities or calculated abundances for non-beneficial and limited personal gain.
- Failure to care for and enhance one's physical possessions.
- Not ensuring that exploitation and valuation of physical resources is consistent with a rational consumership and consumption.
- Irrational waste of any physical resources necessary to support life or commerce.
- Failure to promote the understanding and use of science that does not reduce or eliminate the value and integrity of other domains (e.g., the 7th Domain reduced by *scientism*).
- Generally irrational and exclusive awareness valuation of the physical, which excludes higher realms of contextual value provided by other domains.
- Creation and irrational use of weaponry, including potentially destructive use or control of nuclear energy.

Actualization is an orderly and displayed subtraction from infinity.
Holosophy definition

- Neglect of proper peaceful and productive use of and control of nuclear energy for the common good.
- Denigration of the higher spiritual purpose of mastery and proper utilization of the fundamental physical laws (physics).
- Preventing another's ethical and legal access to any space, time, energy or objects.
- Acting to prevent legal entry, exit, acquisition of, or connectivity to information.
- Travel—either enforced or inhibited, e.g., relocation without consent, mass war-related emigration.
- Destruction of any energy or objects not for a greater good.

VII. 7th Domain: "Conceptual* Source"
- Destroying or inhibiting one's own or another's rational creativity.
- The perpetration of a harmful *un*truth and/or its dissemination.
- Attempts to deny, reduce, or eradicate the spiritual components of Kosmic existence.
- The installing or promoting of preference for lowered standards of ethics and aesthetics ... lesser good made valuable.
- Failure to educate or educating harmfully.
- Propagandizing ... to distort truth and accuracy.
- Demagoguery ... to appeal to sub-rational group ideation and bias.

---

* Thought in the highest/non-material sense—the source of conceptuality or *specified* meaningfulness: i.e., the attributive meaning or *being of knowing*.

Meaning is the selected knowing prior to the symbol, that merely represents it.
  - Holosophy adage

- Hindering personal freedom or its rational exercise through censorious restriction of ideas or speech.
- Compromising higher standards of personal integrity.
- Acting, based on un-reasoning obstruction or denial of all non-material realms: "Kosmos = Cosmos."
- Acting from a blanket invalidation of any possible realm of spiritual agency or even the *idea* that there is an existence of holon/spiritual agent/higher beingness, purpose or design.
- Active denial of the unique *qualitative* nature of life or life sources.
- Developing and indulging a preference for devalued or degraded thought or attitude.
- Denial of personal responsibility for emanating thought, intention, and perception.
- Deceptive inculcation of ideas in other beings with or without force or consent, e.g., brainwashing, subliminal advertising, hypnotic control mechanisms.
- Providing harmful instruction or advice contributing to the diminishing or impairing of any faculty.
- Attacking and/or persistent opposition to the basic philosophy of holosophy or personal transformation, its practices or *any* effective effort to erase sub-rationality and raise human ability and consciousness.
- Harmful or irrational self-abnegation or self-denial; an unwillingness to be a casual, self-determined and accountable agency as holon.
- Irrational displacement of actual persona—"I'm not really important"; "I don't really exist" as sub-rational expiation; suicide to avoid confronting or handling life exigencies.

Change equals actualized potential ...
  -Holosophy maxim

- Deceptive manipulation of context, i.e., "positioning" that seeks to distort, negatively influence or bias accurate perception or information... "fake news" or gossip.
- Ascribing one's personal ambitious or motivation solely to a putative personal and detailed instruction from a deity.
- Failure to keep one's promises or maintain the sustained intention necessary to accomplish a promised result.
- Acting based on displacement of the conceptual into physical realm, i.e., concept confused with symbol or object.

VIII. 8th Domain: Infinite Potential; Supreme Being; "Source of Sources"
- Religious intolerance or sub-rational fanaticism.
- Tolerance of any harmfulness in the name of religion.
- *Mis*placing the 8th domain on various other domains— idolatry, anthropomorphism; "science" as materialism (scient*ism*) when referencing or excluding 8th domain.
- Interfering with non-harmful practices, dicta (beliefs) or accoutrements of any religion.
- Consciously perverting the higher aims of any efforts at raising human consciousness through numinous. (religious) contemplation or practice.
- Trivializing or demeaning honest devotional activity or intent to expand or elevate human consciousness by *any* spiritual means.
- Practicing or instituting a religion *solely* for personal, mercenary or political gain.
- Closing off or preventing any authentic contact with higher spiritual insight or revelation.

> *For all we know, this world is very faulty and imperfect ...;*
> *and was only the first rude essay of some infant deity, who later abandoned it*
> -David Hume, philosopher

- *Enforced* propagation or proselytization of any religious doctrine or practice upon those who are unprepared, unable, or disinclined to understand or accept their principles.
- Self-sacrifice, immolation or suicide to attain political or "religious" ends.
- Falsely ascribing self-serving personal or base political motivations to instructions from any religious text or deity.

Too many pieces of music finish too long after the end...
Igor Stravinsky, composer

Postlogue

It can be seen from a careful review of the previous commentary that the quality of personal ethics correlates directly with post traumatic erasure* as a re-enabled experiencing of novelty, i.e. *freedom* from the compulsive re-enactments, and mental picturing of the past ... and also to *perceive* and give proper emphasis to the uniqueness of *each* domain, and its elements and symbiotes necessary to make the rational choices regarding prioritization and *exchange,* that apparently determine true *ethical* behavior and quality of life across the Kosmic domains.

Additionally, a deeper and contemplative study of Holosophy materials may tend to stimulate or restore even broader personal creative access to elevated and objective norms and value-standards fundamental to the realization of Right Action in the Kosmic Life Game. This, along with increased personal awareness, self-determinism, and ability, is the basic goal of *all* aspects and applications of enhanced awareness in Holosophy and is the expressed Kosmic dedication of purpose for this and all transformative *re*visioning of the fundamentals of Consciousness and its highest cognitive and actualizing capacities.

-R.T.

---

*A note on the typical client-responses associated with erasure: what is normally experienced when an *authentic* erasure, epiphany, or realization occurs, is a momentary (but sometimes protracted) feeling of well-being or even mild euphoria ... it is as if one "gets" the metaphysical Kosmic joke of the revealed *pretense* of "*not knowing,*" i.e., realizing, with a burst of amusement, t*he absurdity* of the holon's contrived and locally "denied familiarity" with its own primal and native creativity, as well as the relief and *joy* in that discovery. In fact, the cascade of insightful inferences characteristic of a successful dialogue, has come to be called, aptly, "the giggle path" ... usually resulting in a *laugh* that is unforced, and spontaneous, but certainly not "required" ... However, the presence or absence of which, *can* be a useful diagnostic indicator of any *actual* "volitional vanishment," or erasure, in dialogue, of the targeted obstacles to optimization.

Part III

Kosmic History and the Primal Mechanism of Sub-Rationality*

*A selected compilation of written and spoken words by the author 1980 to the present.

There is nothing as useless as doing successfully what shouldn't be done at all..."
- Peter Drucker

> *Note to the reader*:
> The following paragraphs have been selected from the author's past writings and lectures. They are not in any historical order and are chosen for their developmental treatment of some of the primary evolving ideas and observations in the subject. They should be viewed and considered in that context.

The deeper source and origins of human aberration have long been a source of both philosophic and psychological speculation. Holosophy's original contribution to that traditional search can be found in other of its publications. (See Volume I of this series and other references in Appendix XIV.)

In the present effort, there has been focus on a general treatment of some of the salient and core theoretical ideas about the genesis and primary aspects of the Kosmology as related to its *domain structure and interactivity*. In earlier sections we reviewed the concept of optimization of choice across all domains, as a useful referential factor in determining objective valuation, and in making the resultant optimizing choices. We now consider some core cosmological aspects of human aberration as an *installed* and unnatural disruption of consciousness and choice, designed to distort, copy and disable the primeval archetypal template built on innate and guiding evolutionary parameters, which each individual uses to selectively frame and establish the rational and ultimately consensual "boundaries of play" for ordinary living ...*

- Briefly stated, its *Galactic* origin consists of a deceptive and *forcefully **implanted** pictured copy* of the actual pattern of the Kosmic Life-Game into the reduced consciousness of the targeted players. To seemingly preserve game continuity

---

*e.g., Fichte, Leibnitz, Hegel, Jung, Whitehead, to name just a few ... plus the earliest Mandalic and Cosmic/historical traditions of Buddhism and Vedanta as well as the ancient Mayans, Egyptians, et al.

> *I am that by which I know I am ...*
> - Ramana Maharshi, Contemplative

from apparent revelatory cessation, the effected holons *freely*, but redundantly, and *under the duress of the implant-trauma* sub-rationally recreate (copy) the Game Pattern to "restore" it after a seemingly *premature, enforced, and erasing revelation*[*] ... apparently to cease to create and co-endow the game in progress, is for all holons, the ultimate Kosmic prohibition!

As a result, post-traumatic *images* from the past (the "subconscious" mind) began to be intrusively *substituted* for the authentic *conceptual game projection* by the holon-players. This occurs through various imposed sub-volitional mental mechanisms, e.g., sub-rational synonyms, picture/concept identification, false reification, and the sub-rational substitution of the "survived" past. This post-traumatic replica is now sub-volitionally needed to *perpetuate the deceptive and implanted the copy* of the games actual and original pattern. However, despite this enduring post-traumatic imposition of implanted and commanded behavior, it is Holosophy's observation that all such apparently sub-volitional causation is actually a *volitional* response to the imposed stress and *created* by the holon ... and can be *un*-created, i.e., *erased* through cognitive, or truth revealing, transformative dialogue or contemplation.

- For any Being, obsessively repeating such a traumatic or implanted past as if it were present, is fundamentally *unethical* since, in so acting, it has abandoned its *present* role and authentic identity in the Life Game. Basically that's a *harmful action*, since one begins to depend on post-traumatic, mentally created experiences, which are redundantly "present" to falsely

---

[*] Just as full awareness of a redundant mental creation or picture causes the holon to cease to create it. The sub-rational (stress induced) perception of the threat to something vital can force an unnecessary sub-aware re-creation of it, which then persists as an unnecessarily "surviving" substitute. Unnecessary in this case because the Kosmic pattern being vastly consensual, is impervious to any individual, or localized and adventitious erasure.

Quality is a range or spectrum of degrees of value..
- Holosophy maxim

represent himself, thereby harmfully abdicating rational and personal Game participation.

In so doing, he's compounding these original harmful acts by compulsively *using repetitively* that which was falsely injected to begin with—with a kind of compelling post-traumatic "survival" errancy. This further isolates him and creates distortions, misunderstandings, etc. of the game itself and his relation to other players. If he, then, *acts* out of those misperceptions, there are further accumulating harmful (contra-survival) actions; and at a critical point, he, being *basically good*, acts *sub*-consciously to *restrain* those harmful actions thereby imposing Success Reluctance (SR), a kind of sub-rational "conscience" that automatically *simulates* other more basic and *rational* limiting mechanisms*. These natural game-sustaining awareness *constraints* are those *copied under duress* to produce when re-activated, the sub-rational, aberrant considerations and *re*straints necessary to *impose* and rationalize the implanted mental copy.

SR is based on those primal, *rational* "game-limit" boundary perimeters, i.e., *thralldom* ... meaning that in order to have a game, *while* building and sustaining its playing field, one *pretends*, game-enthralled, and *projects* the natural ebb and flow of rational gaming opposition. This natural and *changing* progression of eventuality prevents the full erasure (revelatory cessation) of the Game's deeper co-actualized and consensual source. Since this flow of opposition is a valuable and essential condition of the Life-Game, it requires skilled and potentially forceful player interaction. One has a goal that necessitates

---

*The natural "error-limiting" restraints on awareness, causation, and ability necessary to initiate and ensure game reality and progress.

> *To generalize is to be an idiot.*
> \- Wm. Blake, poet

rational countering of opposition to its achievement, while simultaneously providing game sustaining thralldom.

- The *unnatural* interjection of the implant mechanism aside, ... to have an authentic and *convincingly enthralled* game in life requires selectively reducing awareness, and as awareness is reduced you further limit any complete precision of action, resulting in mistakes, and when mistakes are made in the complex and adventurous course of Kosmic Play, others are inevitably harmed. However, instead of immediately erasing that (and *all*) harm, the Being in the Life-Game tends to selectively limit further imprecise harming action, by moving away from the areas where it harmed in error, to seek lesser game involvement! It doesn't *erase* all the originally resulting conditions of harm, because if it did so, from the beginning, there would be no evolving game ... Since a game requires consensual co-experience, there would be no accumulation of existing playing conditions because the mass, space, energy and time involved, also require a time-binding, *consensual* altering continuity! This *co*-creation, by agreement, is not viewed directly, as it actually is (fully restored awareness or revelation of the actual Kosmic consensual-pretense would result in Game erasure)*, but is serially altered into a time-bound continuum (thralldom), assuring a persisting (future) playing field for the game in progress.

The sub-rational mechanism of SR is a redundant, imprinted mental picturing of this primal and game-sustaining "error-limit" mechanism, so it has a convincingly "reasonable" context. All of the elements of the *implanted* Sub-volitional Mind (SM) have this deceptively "rational" basis, due to the

---

*The implant mechanism depends on this truth, to justify installing the deceptive copy!

The essence of knowing is an innate, related, but specified meaningfulness ...
represented by symbol and actualized by intent.
- Holosophy Precept

implant-copied originating primacy of the 7th domain; the generating context of all Kosmic creation and continuity*. This, in effect, gives *implanted* sub-rationally its power! One has post-traumatic reluctance to erase these "grafted on" compulsive *pictures* and impulses because they, unknowingly, are substituted for, and now imitate (copy) the legitimate and actual Life Game pattern! One intends then, sub-volitionally, that these *pictures* are now Reality, including the perceiving "self." If you erase any of these seemingly vital but false pictured identities, from which "you" compulsively, and unknowingly, operate, it seems like a suicidal erasing of "yourself." This is the ancient, but persisting difficulty inherent in both perceiving and explaining the separation of one's authentic character or *persona* from the charged, or trauma-originated, and 'self'-simulating identity-images both stored in, and evoked from the commanding implant-memorial past!

- The *root* causes of SR are to be found, in that past; specifically in incidents of deep pain, confusion, and emotional stress, during which the process of implanted "failure programming" takes place. The mechanism, a post-traumatic additive, works as follows: An individual is always exercising some basic goal-related ability to achieve, or succeed, in the ordinary course and context of daily living ... communicating, driving, working, exercising, etc. ... i.e., a specific capability for being, doing, or having ... which can, obviously, under extreme and painful traumatic circumstances result in variable degrees of unconsciousness ... an individual may lose consciousness in

---

*Subsequent to the traumatically implanted copy of the actual Kosmic pattern, the recovered, now aware, being has to then justify *unethical acting out of* that false copy of its primal Kosmic commitment. This is done by creating synonymic identification of the sub-rational with the rational, e.g., "alone = lonely." This now explains, and makes "reasonable," post facto, the compelling sub-volitional impulses (See Part IV).

> *Cogito ergo sum: Consciousness hence existence.*
> – Descartes (an alternative translation)

an auto collision; a worker may suffer injury on the job; while playing in the backyard, a child may lose consciousness after falling from a tree ... these normative possibilities extend back, less innocently, into primordial times* where traumas were sometimes *used* to inculcate or "implant" belief and behavior modifying *post-traumatic suggestions* and compulsive memorial content. This *installed* used subsequently to both limit and/or use and direct belief and behavior, much like a *post-hypnotic* suggestion has *motive*-force.

- Whatever and whenever the *primary* traumatic event ... the individual, confused with diminished awareness and unable to think rationally, can automatically associated *any* current ability, or activity experienced during the trauma with its pain, loss, suggestive content, and failure! Further, and a seeming paradox, ... can, at the same time, sub-volitionally associate these elements with Survival ... because even under such stress, the holon is surviving, i.e., as *continuing* and still vestigially conscious**, but simultaneously is *unconsciously* identifying survival with *what is being survived,* and restored to consciousness, compulsively copying (re-enacting) it, to survive again!

The result? Because basic *survival* is a primary instinctual impetus of all life-forms, one that will not be ignored under *any* circumstances, and from which an extraordinarily powerful "fail-safe" *solution* is *imprinted,* ... a powerful *sub*-awareness program for "survival" as action (or in-action) and containing *pain* associated *premises*. This "stress-enforced learning" *commands* that to ensure "Survival," the *same* confused and painful viewpoints and activity experienced (as *contra-*

---

* Interesting is a recent book: Humans are not from Earth by Elliot Silver, PhD.
** There is abundant evidence that the "unconscious" mind is, even at the deepest level, *always, to some degree* responsively conscious and aware.

Meaning is the selected knowing prior to the symbol that merely represents it.
                                                    - Holosophy adage

survival defeat) during the trauma, be automatically re-created and *used* as a fixed, outdated, and falsely infallible 'lesson' for responding to any 'similar experiences' in the future ... *despite* its potentially error-prone mis-applications ... and with its multiple negative, personal, social, and biological consequences!

... A deeper and more advanced and explanatory perspective* is that the holon will sub-rationally restrain *any* ability it has used to irrationally harm in the past. Rather than restore that ability when needed to respond to a challenge. So the being actually seeks covertly to *be a victim* rather than restore an ability to *make a victim in* a situation or challenge. One compulsively selects victimhood in the present rather than restore one's native ability to create rational opposition ... and win (harmfully).

- Let's consider some related and generally informative examples from our experimental behavioral-science legacy: traditionally, the behavior modifying sequences and effects of traumatic events described above have been narrowly referred to as "operant conditioning." Countless experiments have been done with animals to demonstrate its occurrence, including one seminal study was conducted by Dr. E. L. Hunt and reported in the Journal of Comparative and Physiological Psychology as early as 1949 ...

In Hunt's experiment, a spasmodic reflex was induced in chicken embryos by subjecting them to the sound of a bell accompanied by a series of electric shocks, while they were still in the shell. After they were hatched, the same chicks responded spasmodically to the bell alone, while a control

---
*More fully examined in ensuing chapters.

> *Objective truth must exist, if some (or any) comparative statements are truer than others.*
> - Holosophy maxim

group which had not been given shocks ignored the sound … showing "survival"-related-imprinting, even at the supposedly unconscious cellular level!

- Another interesting and related experiment put a voracious pike in a tank with minnows, the pike's natural food … but a glass panel was inserted into the tank to prevent any contact. The hungry pike tried repeatedly and unsuccessfully to attack the minnows … after a traumatically extended period, the pike ceased trying! When the panel was removed, the pike … having "learned its (stressed induced post-traumatic) "lesson" … continued to swim harmlessly among the minnows. Obviously, the pike's normal predatory "success" proclivities (instinctual behavioral premises), had been reframed … by the stressfully imprinted/implanted, but survival-associated feeding prohibition.

Similarly, in India, work elephants are implanted with "control training." When very young, the elephants are secured with a heavy chain. As they grow and develop, they "learn" that they cannot move beyond the perimeter allowed by the chain. The chain is then replaced by a thin rope leash which the animal equates with the unbreakable chain and … post traumatically accepting the confined "survival" boundary … is then easily led by its handler. A final example which is said to have inspired the experimental work on "conditioned responses" by the Physiologist I. Pavlov. He had observed early how the famous Russian "Dancing Bears" were trained for local circus performances by leading them over hot coals while music played. Soon, the bears were "dancing" in response to the music alone, without further inspiration from the hot coals.

> *Repeating a word again and again shows that in itself, without a use in a situation, it becomes meaningless.*
> *-Ludwig Wittgenstein, Austrian-British philosopher*

- More recently (2008) an unusual circumstance occurred in East Germany. The government was conducting a biological survey of deer behavior patterns to facilitate conservation planning … scientists on both sides of the former East German border began to study red deer migration patterns, now that the iron curtain fence between the countries was gone. Amazingly, the deer refused to cross the old border into the East. For the deer, the years of "cold war" imprinted stresses and barriers were apparently still very much in place … there remained a "wall in the deer's head" that continued to confine their activity.

So much for animal behavior. Given the added factors of language, its meaning, *semantic* context, and the vastly superior levels of human cognitive and creative capacity …any solution, or stress responsively premised "means to survival," formed (or implanted) sub-rationally as a reaction to threat (and which, in fact, later re-enacts failure) can have similarly conditioned, but more *varied* unintended compulsive (and inhibitory) consequences[*]:

In an important biological sense, a false but deeply "imprinted-solution" to any traumatic event, with its fixed and out-dated context and premises, as well as a deeper reluctance to *restore ability to harm,* abused in the past[**], are now apparently

---

[*] In compelling human terms, the late actor Walter Matthau provided during an interview, a personally vivid anecdotal description of circumstances dramatically "imprinted during and following a serious heart attack he experienced at his home in Hollywood. Subsequent to the attack, Matthau moved from the home but for years after experienced "drive-by palpitations" when even passing close to it. In addition, he recounted how he developed an aversion to the type of water pick he was using when the attack occurred to remove the remnants of some lamb, long favorite food, that he had eaten earlier in the evening. The actor further emphasized that he never again regained his taste for lamb, and habitually avoided thereafter anything associated with the attack.

[**] It is not *personal* survival that is the holon's concern in a primary implant, but the stress imposed avoidance of a total *game-ending* revelation of the actual Kosmic pattern that results in the false copy of the pattern that is then endowed, compulsively, to ensure "game survivability"!

No line should be drawn for eternity... all boundaries are creative perimeters of convenience.
  -Holosophy maxim

"grafted" onto the holon's actual archetypal* 'blueprint' for perceiving, playing, and surviving, the daily "game of life." Since to the sub-rational mind, anything merely "lived through" has rudimentary SURVIVAL value ... and more basically of the supposedly vital implant-copy!

- When clients are first introduced to the concept and mechanism of Success Reluctance, they often try searching their memories to recall experiences which might account for any such present-time patterns of "failure." Most people can easily recall at least one or two painful or embarrassing incidents from childhood, but it is difficult to recall, revive, and confront in full, seminal traumatic incidents ... events during which a complex fabric of irrational core beliefs, fixed ideation, and even aspects of the past identities** which expressed them at the time, were then robotically re-enacted, forever after, as "infallible" personal survival-prescriptions but more importantly for the Life-Game itself!

---

*The existence of "cellular memory" influences on behavior is well documented, e.g. by anomalous behavior experienced following organ transplants, etc. ... but when these imprinted traumatic memories contain false beliefs, formed under stress, and encoded with survival value, their activation and interpretation can cause any of a whole catalog of self- destructive impulses and behavior.

The Cellular DNA holds the encoded blueprint for all biological life. The chemical sequencing of its organic structure contains the genetic code and information which, although unique and personal, only guides, but does *not* fully determine, our physical endowments or our deeper ancestral/archetypal influences and biological heritage ... or our free choices and independent volition.

The traumatic imprinting of this genetic heritage and its after effects is in the form of cellular memories which contain primitive "survival values" ... however, they do not ultimately cause behavior any more than an architect's blueprint *compels* the architect's building choices or decisions...

The life-time accumulation of these childhood (and beyond) responses to memorialized traumatic stress gradually forms a false and *implanted* "selfhood" or mentally pictured ego ... the dissolution of which, through holosophy's cognitive reminiscence, and other systematic techniques of re-ensoulment has been the ultimate transformative aspiration of the great integral traditions of all ages.

**Identity: an assumed role, or projected way of being used by an individual consciousness (or *un*consciousness) to accomplish an objective.

In the quantum universe, we are no longer the robotic automate that classical physics proclaimed us to be ... our minds' matter...

-Henry Stapp, physicist

These roles were present during the original traumatic incident, when identities in the incident were recorded and thereafter re-assumed as a part of a post-traumatic solution to ensure survival. The reason for this, as earlier stated has to do with the awareness-reducing pain, confusion and belief formulation, equated with the fixed and outdated "valuable because survived" belief-content of these incidents.

Obviously, humans, like all living organisms, tend to avoid pain, as contra-survival experience, but at a deeper genetic level, biologically encoded "survival" may require continued retention and primal reenactment of painful events in the form of their re-imposed mental-images and repetitive behavior... This compulsive "repeat-performance" is driven by the assumed but false and hidden "value-added," bio-programmed repetition of the trauma, to "survive" similar events or deeper and more basically, to *preserve the game itself*!

Transformative Re-Education:
Eliminating Success Reluctance

Fortunately, the decisions, beliefs, falsely assumed identity-roles, and other post-traumatic "solutions" underlying Success Reluctance can be gently and systematically located, re-examined, and extinguished, i.e. erased ... freeing the individual to pursue rational goals in all areas of life with restored self-determinism, enthusiasm, confidence and actual success as realized and *rational* goal-achievement.

What is word knowledge but a shadow of wordless knowledge.
-Kahlil Gibran

The process of complete removal or "clearing"* of these "dramatized" stressed-conditioned (*sub*-rational) response mechanisms of self-sabotage, which result in the unwanted "failure-conditions" of our daily lives requires time and professional assistance, naturally ... but to begin to notice and become gradually, and more fully aware through both transformative re-education, counseling, and informed self-observation of seemingly aberrant impediments imposed by compulsive *re*experiment of past pain enforced belief and behavior . . . Not as a supposed inherent *drive to succumb* or "death instinct," but as a powerful implanted impulse to perpetuate the life-game itself, deceptively *mis*appropriated by the sub-rational mind. All such Success Reluctant behavior is pattern-like, and with re-imposed markers** symptomatic of the original feelings and impulses that, *re-imposed now,* are obsessively sabotaging one's well-being in a misguided effort to survive, i.e., to preserve the *game itself*!

Obviously, no one with *full* awareness would rationally and knowingly choose to install and exercise behavior that is, at the same time, obviously counterproductive, unpleasant, and damaging to oneself and other domains of Life!

The first step to *restore* that sabotaged awareness (Transformative Re-Education) is to begin to identify, access, and directly view, in a systematic program of *cognitive optimization,* the hidden survival "premiums" and self-negating beliefs underlying Success Reluctance with as much accuracy and objectivity as possible. Using remedial dialoguing

---

*Holosophy uses this common, computational term to mean the systematic accessing, de-conditioning, and erasure, through explorative dialoguing, and Transformative Re-Education, of sub-rationally memorialized, responses to past traumatic events, Much as a computer program is "cleared" by de-bugging!
**See Part IV

Repetition with full awareness is transformative.
-Holosophy Precept

techniques that re-enable one to begin to think and observe "outside the box," or the envelope of sub-rational "selfhood" … we gradually reach deeper levels of inspection and insight and are finally able to volitionally cease to obsessively choose and re-enact a primal *implanted* and true identity eclipsing … past re-imposed *in* the present.

With targetted dialoguing, we assist the client to restore personal responsibility* and confident causativeness over all such self-destructive mental "feedback" and thereby eliminate it. Noticing the success-obstructing surface indicators (unwanted life-conditions) is a vital first step to the eventual full access, ownership, and "erasure" of all self-sabotaging programs and premises with their restraint of the free exercise of one's abilities.

Applying Holosophy dialoguing methods which employ a cognitive/transformative tracing back to the earliest basic, and formative traumatic limit-imprinting episodes … we can then recognize, own, and re-create fully the primary sources *and* dynamics of such behavior … and systematically *erase* (*cease* to create) the "persisting" unwanted behavioral states, conditions, and beliefs that are projected from them. When this targeted and insightful re-experiencing is achieved, one can, with restored ability, choicefully *extinguish, and stop re-enacting,* the post-traumatic imprint … experience a profound sense of relief; and, if the behavior is noticed in another, one is *now able* with greater equanimity, compassion, and understanding … to deal with (rationally *counter* and not resist) that "problematic" person or situation *more* effectively.

*Defined in Holosophy as … an inherent ability to cause, or to refrain from causing any act…and the willingness to acknowledge fully the personal ability to be truly self-determined, i.e., to be natively at cause and *sourse of* any act of implementation.

Is perception basically conceptual? ... perception is demonstrably a creative act of consciousness, and that which is sourced by consciousness is essentially of consciousness ... and consciousness-dependent ...
-Holosophy precept

In the most basic sense, irrational Success Reluctance is a system of false confusion-solving responses and premises implanted or traumatically *"grafted" on to* the Cosmic pattern of existence as an endless, post-traumatic command to "survive" as, and within; a debilitating and isolating pain-enforced life-substitute ...

These ancient and fixed failure-patterns are sub-rationally equated with, copy, and feed, leech-like, on that *authentic* deep structured, "soul-encoded" template for living ... and are stored within the implanted collection of surrogate "selves" and data that comprise the earlier false Kosmic pattern replication and from which the later reminding events are sub-rationally re-enacted to "ensure survival." Not as mere continuity of an *existing self*, but with a deeper false and ultimate *gaming* priority, intended to falsely *restore, copy,* and forever maintain the seemingly threatened Kosmos itself*!

Basically, holosophy addresses this problem by attempting, through dialogue, to increase the willingness of the individual to fully and *gradually* confront *all* domains of existence,

---

*An objection sometimes raised to the basic ability limiting or constraining aspect of Success Reluctance (SR) is the case in which extraordinary ability is destructively "unleashed" in the service of apparently contra-survival ends or purposes. The "evil genius" examples, billionaire misers, robber barons, totalitarian empire builders ... Hitler, Stalin, Mao, et al. seem to act destructively without limitation, or consequence.

However, even these apparent exceptions, the *sub*-rational or unethical aspects of that ability - exercise, typically and ultimately, takes a terrible toll on the personal level of awareness, quality of life of the miscreant. **Witness both Hitler and Napoleon's disastrous invasions of Russia. Even Stalin's apparent final dominance ended up with him as a physically infirm, isolated, and friendless paranoiac ... evil purpose** is *never* without consequence!

In the cases of destructive use of exception ability, a careful inspection and analysis reveals sub-rational restraints on logical analysis, goals, and target selection, result invariably in sociopathic opinion or impulse, and associated psychosomatic dysfunction. All are in evidence where unusual levels of ability are focused on or harnessed by sub-rationally distorted impulses, e.g., where one domain has had *compulsive* domination over others.

The natural, Kosmically patterned, error-limited impairment of misused or "harming" ability when transferred post-traumatically to the sub-rational mind, results in the *irrational* limitation, or a or a narrow and ofensive heightening of emotion and awareness, e.g. compulsive glee, with *reduced* ability to focus rationally, i.e., *Success Reluctance!*

If you argue for your limitations, you usually win ... and get to keep them.
-Anonymous

both individually and inclusively, and become aware of the differentiating features of actual domain exchange potentials versus subverting post-traumatically *placed* mental *pictures*. The Being then begins to see the optimizing multi-domain *ethical* value of erasing, or *ceasing to create*, any and all mental pictures that are falsely pretending to be an authentically present reality. Especially those of *being* a substantive, post-traumatic, "Self," compulsively repeating *past pictured* experience, as "survival solutions" ... Traumatic content which carries the implanted conviction that if you erase them, you're destroying the very universe itself; ... the ultimate taboo! If you identify the authentic Life Game with traumatic mental *pictures* of the past that enact the *resistance* mechanism of "I can't look at that, it will reveal and destroy the illusion I depend on to survive!" then you've sub-rationally identified post-traumatic copies of past experience, with the real, *truly novel*, and *non*-"pictured" present ... succumbing again to the impulse to project, *endow*, and inhabit, a false, implanted, *"surviving" copy* of the actual pattern of the Kosmos.

- Let's now consider some specifics of an actual self-sabotaging case mechanism, e.g., the sub-rational phenomena of "procrastination..." The basic ability or potential for *rational postponement* derives from a basic truth or conceptual potential, i.e., the capacity to delay your activities and selectively not do things in order to act rationally, not harm, and/or accomplish goals. This requires that one choose, be decisive, and be self-motivated; each a rational and basic ability. However, if we sub-volitionally copy (and replace) that capacity, by making the disability-associated word "procrastinate" mean the same in execution, as its rational counterpart, i.e., the ability to optimally *delay or defer* gratification...this sub-rational *substitution* accomplishes the post-traumatic objective of equating different

...correlation is not causation ... nor is to forgive ... to sanction...
-Holosophy precepts

meanings synonymically to *impose* the *sub*-rational *framing* of the compulsive act or condition! *Deferring* action selectively *is* rational. *Procrastination* is an aberration that *pictures sub*-optimal *in*action, and then, obsessively both justifies and *compels* its *re*-enactment...To continue "forever," the success-reluctant inhibition of *delay-ability* by a perpetually "survived" painful past *plus* the compelling, implant-created *copy* of the Kosmic!

If you now use that ability, to defer an action, rationally, you may experience its *sub*-rational *reminding* surrogate, the *added* and *disabling* symbol; the post-traumatically defined synonym! ... I rationally conceive and intend the *deferring* of action or "delay," but *sub*-rationality interjects as a disabling procrastination! Delay itself, doesn't have to be irrational, but procrastination *is irrational* delay, "grafted" onto the "present" as a *dis*abling re-enactment, imposed by the sub-rational mind to *limit* some ancient misused and "harming" *ability to defer action.*

Assume one intends to "delay" or "defer" because success in the game of life requires rational flexibility regarding timing your actions. One must be able to evaluate *any* delays *relative importance* as an action or inaction, to be *able* to effectively delay! But, the ability to delay optimally, can become sub-rationally *displaced and* identified with its sub-rational *synonym*, "procrastination." The actual intended meaning of the *rationally* sourced concept of delay *transfers* to "procrastination." Suddenly "you" are procrastinating, and in the grip of an obsessive delaying tactic. A tactic that, in degree, harms all the other domains and seems to have confusing and compelling power over *you.* You seem dominated by this compulsive mechanism and apparently helpless in

In order to break out of a prison, one must first confess to being in a prison.
-Wilhelm Reich, MD

its grip. But actually its power comes from your own native *conceptual ability* to delay, while failing to see the distinction between that *rational* conceptual delay, and re-enacting the usurping and synonymically imposed *hesitation* of sub-rational procrastination (*irrational* delay).

Without realizing it, you're forced out of character, and compulsively assume the false identity of the trauma-driven "procrastinator." Now you're "it," and are unknowingly re-enacting this irrational substitute identity with its sub-rational compulsiveness, which is also *harming the domains* by imposing on the present, an equivalent forgotten, *substitute* agenda from the *past* ... This *mis*-use then tends to become habitual and leads the holon into the *effect* side of the sub-volitionally enacted equation in which to "balance-the-scales," it now *acts to receives* the self-imposed, retributive "karmic" effects, to restrain the rational *countering* ability to "harm." However, this is accompanied by a *sub*-rationally imposed "victimized" dramatization with a protestation of *receiving* the supposed undeserved, uncaused and *blamable* "injustice."

- So we see that, from a transcendent Source (7th domain), each being's authentic co-actualizing conceptualization of life and livingness, there emerges *all* life experience ... as *eight* domain Kosmic Play... But when that playfulness and action is traumatically copied and *replaced* by a hidden, *implanted* counterpart, which is then automatically and *sub*-volitionally created, energized, and obeyed, we have a *displacing sub*-volitional mind! Of course, to *obsessively* re-enact the past, we *also* have the consequent, and subsequent, mechanism called SR which itself, is the holons' *sub*-rational and misguided post-traumatic attempt at "ethical" *restraint* of the resultant sub-rational *harming*. Such false restraint being a disabling

> *Among the great things which are found among us,*
> *the existence of nothing is the greatest.*
>
> -Leonardo da Vinc

overlay itself, results in even *greater* harm, reducing incremental betterment across the Kosmic Domains!

- Apparently *all* post-traumatic ability-limiting intricacies result from an unnecessary or "extra" and "thin" *restraining* projection and *redundant overlay* of the fundamental archetypal pattern behind Kosmic existence. The essence of this primal pattern we term Error-Limit, which, again, is the *rational* limitation progression postulated by all beings to obtain a persisting universal game-recreation in which the thralldom of holon co-existence and participation is convincingly actualized. The SM is a *pictured* spin-off, or *implanted post-traumatic mockery* of that rational error-limited game activity, *distorting* play, perception, and participation in the actual gaming pattern of Kosmic existence.

- ... The challenge is to apply meticulous remedial self-observation and awareness, within the broader philosophic framework of an effective Holosophy praxis*. Using this heuristic knowledge of how the total mind is structured provides effective technical guidelines and address to *erasing* the *sub-rational* mind. This requires also, an awareness of all the twists

---

*One of the basic epistemic components of holosophy is hol*ism:* the idea that the universe is essentially reducible to *cognitive wholes*; ideas, rather than material *things*. All existence has a consciousness involved and *derived* primary nature.

A *holistic* or "top-down universe" is one in which primary conceptuality is more fundamental than its projected *forms*, which are *derived from it as combined conceptualities*. Ultimately, all existence is a single unified, interconnected whole comprised of 8 *sub*-projections or domains, which are interconnected to afford the interactive exchanges between areas of play ... that is actually their primal purposeness: Kosmic play! Holosophy terms this *"agentive kosmopsychism"*; game-enabling constraints on the player agencies and domain projected conditions of play. This view seems maximally consistent with the holosophy truth functions (see Appendix I), having the most kosmically fundamental elements consistent with the grand and primal vedantic "Lila" or *God's Game* as its *kosmo*psychist centerpiece ... in essence, holosophy elaborates and expands a passive *pan*pychism to include the active and creative nature of holons as agentive, universal, irreducibly conceptual *player projectionists*, i.e., consensually and divinely coordinated, *kosmo*psychists!

> *Physical brain states are* not *intentional (about anything) but* mental *states are ... a vital substantive distinction.*
> -Holosophy canon

and turns and resistive tactics holons employ to sustain a "valued" sub-rationally, and to *avoid* confronting (and erasing) it! Paradoxically, the mechanics of this resistance spring out of a distortion of the rational desire to *maintain* the Life Game, a a basic life *instinct*... a natural game-enabling impetus which requires a tactical and *selective un*awareness, of the game-*preserving* thralldom, and also gradually increasing awareness of it as a natural game-*enabling* and *containing* Kosmic progression!

Trance is the *sub*-volitional *mentally-pictured* side of this primal rational and conceptual thralldom. So, if we intend thralldom and sub-rationally get trance, that reduction of consciousness is a self-sabotaging mockery of a primal mechanism that *rationally* generates an enthralled, and *playfully un*aware *display* of existence, *from a Kosmic essence!* When we *truly* see that false and disabling overlay of harmfully redundant mental-imagery *for the "invasive" substitute it actually is* ... we cease to create (erase) it ... and the restored novelty and bliss of the Real is suddenly, surprisingly, and sublimely evident!

-R.T.

Part IV

Sub-Rational Synonyms

as a Hidden Causal Link to Enacting Aberrant Behavior

> *A symbol has mass, meaning, and transferability all at once ... and is a slippery thing at best... at worst, evil incarnate!*
> - Holosophic observation

Sub-Rational Synonyms
A brief reprise with example lists.

In this brief data-summary we re-examine a theoretical explanation of *how* the post-traumatic triggering mechanism produces synonymic mis-definition—with the resulting generic sub-rational *indicators and behaviors*. Two basic questions are posed:

> How does a mind with a traumatically reduced *minimal* awareness exert a seemingly permanent and compelling *post-traumatic* influence over the authentic *person's* future belief and behavior?

> How does the rationally habituated transition path from concept, to usage, to perception and action, get so deviously "hijacked" to impose, subtly justify, and enact sub-rational compulsion, and ability limitation?

Since a Holon is basically a *non*-material *meaning creator*, it is, in essence, non-existent in terms of the *physical universe*. However, the closest *existing thing* to a Holon is a *symbolized* meaning or concept (word.) *The symbolic is the communication enabling* cognitive modality composed of mass (a substantive, representing, entity, e.g., a word or thing), cognitive relevance or *meaning,* and mobility or *transmissive capacity*, all at once!

When the Holon conceptually "places" and thereby creatively *attributes meaning* to the external forms of life and existence (perceives), it does so by cognitive *combining of* significances, or concepts. This aggregate formation of conceptual assemblages

> A person's worth enemy can't wish on him what he can think up himself
> - Yiddish saying

(qualia*) is necessary to endow and experience the "*be*ables" or perceptual *conditions* of existence. These resultant *combined conceptualities* are then *experienced* much like the "whole" apparently "seamless" image-*constructing* grouping of pixels on a computer or television screen. The images being *distinct* from the combined pixels!

A *sub*-rational semantic perspective is a "pictured viewpoint" from the past, which *contains* a fixed and specific, *trauma-associated*, but seemingly essential** "meaning" for a word or symbol. Such interposed viewpoints have command-value over the experience of the Holon, because they emulate, albeit redundantly, the way a holon creates its world; i.e., by postulating and signifying *personal qualia* as *combined* conceptualization. Priority is given to those actualizations which seem, through mutual agreement of all holons, to be most essential to the *consensually displayed continuity* of the actual pattern of the Kosmos.

The repository of past trauma-linked perspectives in totality; i.e., the *Sub*-rational mind, is that part of the mind which tends to *compulsively*, and with no awareness of *abstracting*, symbolize or "picture" rather than directly perceive (conceptually postulate), as does the rational or analytical "mental" faculty of the holon. The *sub*-rational mind acts *as if it were* the constant present, and operating, holon (the *rational,* postulating, agency of awareness) but is actually *displacing it* with fixed, pain-associated *meanings* from the past without rational and *present* contextual referencing. This *fixed* post-traumatic context becomes objectified as a *substitute representation* of a "survival" experience, i.e., a sub-

---

*Holosophy uses the term to mean projected cognitive "wholes" or universals, e.g., redness, hardness, and other "gestalts" of actualization, which themselves *combine* in hierarchic states as specified particulars to form the "projected holism" of experience.

** The analytical mind of the holon has the perpetual challenge of explaining aberrant behavior, i.e., the periodic intervention in consciousness of sub-rational meaning and impulse.

> ... Evil is a distorted Good ... reduced and destructively redefined and trivialized as *sub*-rationally endowed intent.
> - Holosophy principle

volitionally activated and perpetually "surviving" *past mental-image*, now *replacing*, and distorting the present!

For example, if a holon in an ordinary moment of solitude "experiences" (i.e., rationally postulates an existentially projected conceptually) "aloneness," and a very similar but yet *different pictured* meaning (a sub-rational perspective) "loneliness" makes a simultaneous but unnoticed and compulsive appearance in the holon's awareness. The holon, given the false survival-priority of the triggered post-traumatic perspective, mistakenly endows it; and assumes redundant attribution of meaning is validly *present* , and *perceiving through it**, feels "lonely."

As has been referenced earlier, the Holon's ancient pain-associated but seemingly *essential mental copy* of the actual pattern of existence was installed** under extreme duress and used to counter the false revelation, and apparent erasure of the primal source of the game itself with an unnecessary and redundant mentally pictured *post-traumatic replication*. The holon thus falsely assigns validity and *existence generative* capacity to a mentally pictured and *synonymically* substituted meaningfulness, i.e., a *symbol or word*. This mistakenly *endowed substitution* is in fact the holon's sub-rational attempt to explain and justify aberrant post-traumatic belief and behavior. This sub-conscious compulsion to repeat the traumatic *past* with its fixed records of word, meanings, and sensations, becomes a *mentally pictured* substitute for actual living...a stale and implanted copy of the Kosmos!

---

*With a sub-rational fixedness, it dictates the experiencing of the *compulsive* side of the associated pairing no matter what the intended meaning. The holon thus creates a surrogate "case-contour" universe with a subtly displaced significance or word associations which "commands" present awareness to re-experience the past as "perpetual survival" ....

**The total Kosmos, or its projection from a primal guiding actualizing pattern, doesn't depend on any *single* holon, but on a consensual co-creating *aggregation of* all *holon-participants* (reality).

> *Dialoguing simply removes fixed sub-rational significances from a past location, domain, or activity so that its actual conceptual memory can be restored and used newly as cognitive familiarity with the Kosmic playing field.*
> -Holosophy Tenet

Thus an errant and *mis*-signified "synonym" can interject and act as a false "command" to experience a sub-rational universe of substituted and enforced signification (symbol), e.g., *aloneness equals* loneliness, as a seemingly legitimate and authentic perception, but actually framed and "commanded" by a false trauma-associated context from the past. *This distorting feedback then overlays and is substituted for the real and intended meaning or consensus thralldom of the Life Game play in progress.*

Differentiating through dialogue the rationally intended concept from the displacing synonymic overlay (symbol) devalues, repetitively *de*constructs and erases, the mis-defined connection to the holon; by recognizing and rationally *re*framing all false post-traumatic referencing of the *past "as if" it were the present*.

By the volitional cessation through cognitive dialogue, of the superimposed sub-rational post-traumatic attribution of "loneliness" upon its experiencing of solitude, the holon restores or rational assignment of meaning from a *present* analytical context and is then just objectively *alone*, but not *subjectively* "lonely." The restored capacity of the holon to perceive directly, and not via a past, *symbolic* "self-identity," but now, from a free, authentic, *non*-material, and *novelty actualizing* viewpoint, ... a pure, transformative, and *present* witnessing!

Present causation is motivated by idealized future perspectives.
-Holosophy Canon

Synonymic Dishabituation Drill
Short Form I

Appended is a representative list of common sub-rational synonyms that may be used in various conceptual/word differentiation and clarification drills, a basic example of which follows:

1. Understand fully through dictionary use, the meaning of ... sub-rational or "*re*active" indicator, concept, symbol, mental image picture, word, synonym, perception, game, thralldom, and postulate. (See also Holosophy source materials, Appendix XIV).

2. Fully research and define any applicable (life difficulty or 'confusion' related) pair (A= B) of synonyms to a state of relieved redefinition and understanding. (Client must understand the meaning of the sub-rational as distinct from the rational and that all words (as symbols) are multi-ordinal*.

3. Ask the questions below in sequence to cognitive closure:

    1. "Is (A) always (B)? Is (B) always (A)?

    2. "How is (A) similar to (B)?

    3. "How is (A) different than (B)?

    4. "What variable meaning of (A) or (B) has been obscured or excluded?"

    5. "Does any word in the pair *bring about* the meaning of the other word?" How?

4. Review each side of the list of synonyms for any 'undesired characteristic', then determine and define fully, as in Step 1, the

*Infinitely graduated shades of meaning and application

Power is the degree of capacity to act, construct, or make known....
-Holosophy Canon

Synonymic Dishabituation Drill
Short Form I (continued)

    irrationally significant or triggering synonym within the pair and then do Step 2 above.

5. Introduce in a dialogue any persisting Sub-rational Indicators occurring on any list word or pair and tracing back to earlier use or instance of misdefinition, then complete Step 2 and complete to a new and certain realization (cognitive closure).

6 Assess each side of the synonym word list for "desired characteristic," define synonym, and do Step 2. To a fully and newly relieved state of awareness (erasure of any hidden irrational equivalence).

7 Any unyielding review of symbolic pairings can be usefully introduced into the cognitive optimization dialogue procedures described in other publications (see Appendix XIV).

Note: The following lists of synonyms are intended as representative pair samplings from Holosophic case research and are not presented as fixed in any absolute sense ... Student or client is encouraged to research for themselves the many nuanced synonymic variables of mis-defined meanings applicable to their own life experience.

The experiential patterns of Kosmic order that generate the cosmos, can usefully be thought of as archetypal templates which coordinate Consciousness at Large with that order by reduction of the quantum wave-function, which brings about and extracts actual eventuality from... mere probability ... the loom and fabric of meanings made substance ...

*Inviting holons to inhabit and animate material objects or processes is a pivotable marker in the great consensual **curve of descent** of the Kosmos.*

-Holosophy Conjectures

Sub-Rational Synonyms (selected list)

Here is a selected list of synonyms. One of the words has a sub-rational implication. The challenge is to recognize the contextual shift that diminishes the intended meaning distinction and makes it sub-rationally identical in meaning and intent.

Abandon - depart	Condition - Intention	Game - combatancy
Ability - compulsion	Consequences - contribution	Gradient - portion
Absence - loss	Comply - obey	Have - own
Acknowledge - agree	Correlation - causation	Hierarchic - elite
Assertive - aggressive	Contextual - historical	Help - charity
Adventure - adversity	Commitment - onus	Hidden - absent
Accepted - commanded	Deprive - curtail	Hubris - pride
Alert - cautious	Desire - require	How - create
Assist - displace	Direct - ruthless	History - context
Avoid - flinch	Destiny - heritage	Illusion - deception
Absent - hidden	Delay - procrastinate	Imaginal - pictorial
Act - react	Duplication - simulation	Integrity - aggression
Alone - lonely	Emotional - sentimental	Isolation - privacy
Automatic - robotic	Enacted - intended	Intrude - enter
Almost - never quite	Enemy - opponent	Imagine - Lie
Attribute - blame	Existing - surviving	Know - think
Boundary - restriction	Enlightenment - uninvolvement	Knowledge - data
Belief - conviction	Ethical - expedient	Kind - indulgent
Brain - mind	Explain - describe	Keen - piercing
Buy - own	Free - reckless	Kinetic - explosive
Become - achieve	Future - fate	Map - territory

Sub-Rational Synonyms (continued)

Beauty - likeability
Can't - won't
Cautious - alert
Charity - entitlement
Capacity - compulsion
Need - require
Notice - appraise
Never - usually not
Nothing - vacuum
Obligation - onus
Own - command/control
Origin - start
Originate - replicate
Opponent - enemy
Order - sequence
Pain - suffering
Pause - waiting
Penalty - punishment

Form - essence
Fixed - stable
Filtered - contextual
Gestural - insincere
Gestalt - seemingness
Playful - superficial
Preference - prejudice
Pretend - falsify
Pralittive - elitist
Quanta - qualia
Reject - respond
Related - connected
Refrain - resist
Realize - regret
Ruthless - efficient
Rule - command
Repetitive - boring
Responsible - blameworthy

Mass - aggregation
Meaning - implication
Master - conquer
Menacing - powerful
Metaphor - description
Selected - imposed
Sentimental - sensitive
Spontaneous - impulsive
Stable - fixed
Survival - existing
Trustworthy - infallable
Transform - translate
Thralldom - trance
Unwilling - unable
Unknown - mystery
Vacuum - plasma
Volition - impulse
Whole - aggregate

Holosophy Terms in General Usage
(Basic and Advanced)*

Intentionality	Subtraction from Infinity	Logic, Truth, Value
Entropy	Pretence	Coherence (and de-)
Sinularity	Deconstruct	Correspondence
Multiverse	Post modern	Pragmatic
Increment	Reductionism	Best Explanation
Identity	Value	Knowingness
Metaphysics	Calculus of optimization	Chaos Theory
Kosmos	Perseity	Triad
Dimension	Transformative acceptance	Quantum entanglement
Matrix (mandala)	Rational choice	Dichotomy
Paradox	Dialectic idealism	Polarity
Ambiguity	Panpsychism	Event Horizon
Absurdity	Aesthetics	Butterfly Effect
Karma	Gesture	combined conceptuality
Kubit	true-witnessing	emergent
information	Cognitive closure	actual pattern
Process	reification	semantic/syntactic
Brain states	abstraction	zero not physical vacuum
Concresence	reality	inference cascade
Optimization	Potentia	Black Hole
Agency	Actualization	Post-traumatic
Holon/Holos	Revealed pretense	unwarranted expectation
"its from bits"	Selective unawareness	duality/non-dual
Consciousness	Entity/entification	Thralldom/enthralled
Template/form	Cosmogony	Psychic Grid
Entelechy	Imaginal	Revealed Pretence
archetype	Occasion/instantiation	Prehension
Lila	Cycle	Subtractive knowing
Zero-sum	Sub-rational	Epistemic
Pervade	*Dis*create/erase	Ontic
Field no particle	Infimity	Telic
Symmetry	Symbol	Synchronicity
Order	Concept	Metasymbolic
Universal/particular	Free/determinist	Item as domain element

*Holosophy may have special usage for many of these terms which are explained in page notations as introduced and applicable and are useful as topics of group discussions.

A brief summary statement of Holosophy cognitive and Philosophical researches to date ...

The soul can be given a scientific meaning as one's immediate perception of one's coherent, uncollapsed wave-function.
R. Rucker, mathematician

I think consciousness will remain a mystery ....
Edward Witton, physicist

Compendium

Finally, let's examine, in capsule, an overview of sub-rational belief and behavior ... and attempt to provide a current summary perspective as to its ultimate source and content:

Holosophy basically holds that all human aberration is traceable to a primal or core sub-rational Template which is a stress-formed post-traumatically imposed mental-image copy, or memory trace, substituting for the actual archetypal* pattern of existence; itself a kind of innate "mandalic" paradigm. An intrinsic pattern which, is central to guiding, but *not* determining, each Holon's authentic persona, intention, activity, and character formation, while living** fully, as a Kosmic player participant.

*Archetype: To restate its holosophy meaning and usage... The a priori (conceptual) guiding potential for symbolization; sometimes refers to (and is confused with) the primary conceptual representation, or the symbol itself: Holosophy uses the term to refer to an *innate*, signification, which when projected as a particular meaningfulness, is the source of all substantive representations, or symbols.

**When overwhelmed by the exigencies of living, a being tends to lose full sense of Kosmic playerhood, its natural connection to it, and responsibility for it - slipping into sub-rational semi-consciousness ... a repository of stress formed memorial images containing past sensations, impulses, beliefs, and surrogate identities ... which deceptively replicate the Holon's natural persona, and is then re-imposed to compel repetition of sub-volitional past "survival" behavior. Holosophy holds that this total accumulated traumatic past is *designed* to mentally preserve, simulate and activate *a copy, overlapping and displacing* the actual conceptual pattern of existence.

> *How "something is" or what its state is, is an illusion ... It may be a useful illusion for some purposes, but if we want to think fundamentally we must not lose sight of the essential fact that it is an illusion ...*
> *-- Lee Smolin, quantum cosmologist*

To reveal, re-appropriate, and re-ensoul, the actual lifegame template ... one must expose the errant departures from it, and erase the redundant *re*active mental-image additives encrusted on it, which is essentially the goal of Holosophy Dialoguing ...

When the Holon falsely copies its own character under extreme duress*; it then tends to confuse - or "fuse" - itself with that substitute character-image! Subsequently, "its" beliefs, activities and impulses tend to be directed by a duplicate, and false surrogate ego, formed under duress as a *"post-traumatic" copy* of its true and actual persona (*original agency* capacity, and purposes).

In essence, the sub-rational mind is the traumatically pictured and multi-layered encrustation of that core belief template, which research has shown is each holon's redundant pain and stress-enforced *copy* of the actual archetypal pattern of Kosmic existence ... an innate formativeness that was originally co-engineered to provide the natural limitations, and opponencies necessary to play a game. A *Kosmic game* of mutually enthralled and ultimately benevolent, recreational display-activity.

That emergent pattern of co-existent intent essentially actualizes the primal "rules of the game," and with tacit selectivity, projects *dialectically* a universe of serial "plus/minus" dualities, eventualities unfolding variously through time as a living Kosmic Template ... a celestial algorithm that describes how the Kosmos displays itself as a game. A vast recreation then enfolds, with its rules, purposes, goals, intentions, universal barriers and organized structure (the 8 domains), all based on agreed-upon, game-

---

*Erasure is the capacity of the person to volitionally cease to create any sub-volitional mental imagery, when perceived and *realized* as redundant, unwanted, emotional, or sub-optimally destructive. This is based on the deeper holosophic insight that all persisting mental-images are created by the being itself and if created, can be optimally and volitionally un-created (erased).

True meditative practice and the transcending actualizations of Art are the metaphoric celebrations of and access to the Sublime.
-Holosophy Canon

determinate archetypal categories and dichotomies, with their projected, co-perceived, and enthralled actualizations.

A Kosmic pattern is thus tacitly adopted by all Holons, to creatively co-actualize purpose through time ... Goals and identities in cyclical opposition are projected to move freely (with an intentional game-enabling limitation) in a serial cosmic pathway. However, the dynamic rules of the Kosmos have a *designed* order and proportionality of manifestation. As in chess, there are progressively tactical events, daily purposes and exchanges; and an overall strategic intent with end-game objectives ... There is apparent local goal completion and finality. Then, after each series of ended game-cycles, there is projected a new game perspective. Consistent with a basic purpose and with a Kosmic cascade of countering, or oppositional, progression; provides *game sustaining* vectors, goals, and identities ... ad infinitum.

As each Holon-Player moves through a succession of solving and counter-solving game purposes and identities, there occurs, because of necessary and *de*volving ability-limitation*, sub-optimal error, and a resultant *self*/limitation to correct its harmful effects. This error-*limit* factor ensures the cumulative and progressive *variation and continuity* of the Kosmic "Game at Large". Resulting, is a pattern of existence which has a fabric of serial goals that proceed through time one after the other, but are connected logically. The logical and thematic connection between the descendant goals, consists of projected and reified prime archetypal oppositions (be, do, have, plus-minus) which express the dialectic gaming-themes of existence, and emerge from its innate conceptual source ... the 7th domain.

---

*The original game establishing rules, conditions, and parameters require gradual awareness and *ability reduction* to avoid *premature* game-revelation and erasure.

> Quantum theory provides a superb description of physical reality on a small scale yet it contains many mysteries. Without doubt, it is hard to come to terms with the workings of the theory, and it's particularly difficult to make sense of the kind of "physical reality - or lack of it - that it seems to imply for our world ...
> Sir Roger Penrose, physicist

The corruption of the game, by apparent forcefully deceptive interventions*, at a primordial stage of play by those who opposed, or were trying to dominate from outside the "game in progress" ... tricked the Holon into creating, under traumatic duress, a *sub-rational act of irrational game-preservation*, and substituting a *pictured copy* of the actual game pattern, including its own original volition, *self*hood, and character. The Holon then *endows*, and is sub-rationally entranced and *led* by that falsely injected game-copy! *Thus, the holon sub-rationally transforms the knowing illusion and benevolent pretense of thralldom, into the unknowing delusion and lie of a trance* ... by obsessively endowing that pictured and *implanted pattern copy*, through the same window (first domain) of creative meaning and value through which it, and each holon-player, endows the actual Kosmos!

The point of holosophy's knowledge and practice is to inquire into and *discard* that *whole* distorting and unnecessarily *addictive re*-creation ... to fully *de*construct it through dialogue, gradually but ultimately recognizing all of its aberrant shifts, shapes and complexities. The ultimate optimizing objective is to finally erase, *or cease to create* the implanted "self" *image and motive* that falsely simulates and "protects" the redundant "survival" *copy* of the ultimately *actuality of* Pattern that both generates and projects the Kosmos ...

This emerging insight "restores" the Holon's true character as *Persona* - Player, as the manifest and distinct actualizing agency

---

*This incident of unconfrontable "erasing" force contains revelatory input about the creative consensual limitation committed to, at the inception of game ... To avoid a seeming *forced revelation* which would spoil that, and suspend all, "*game*" *enabling* thralldom, the Holon in a reduced state of awareness, unnecessarily and *pictorially recreates* (copies) its natural self-imposed state of "tacit" limitation and obsessively *re*imposes it, in order to ensure the game is not erased by a "disenthralling" and unethical revelation of its actual formation construction and reality.

Could kosmic dark matter and energy be the transcending minus *perimeter enabling selectively the plus of material existence?*
-Holosophy conjecture

between the 1st and 7th domains ... the window of non-material personal optimizing volition *through which* all projection of specified conceptuality is made manifest.

Inter-domain exchanges are made possible because all domains have resonant aspect potentialities of all *other* domains contained within them. Induced post-traumatic confusion of these domain-exchange capacities and distinctions, further contributes to the formation and continuity of the sub-rational mind*, which is basically the 7th domain's knowing capacity *redundantly copied*, projected, and reified as an aberrant substitute-reality for the "revelation threatened" game in progress!

Finally, and, most essentially: To metaphysically "stage," ethically source, and perpetually control an enduring and consensual *Kosmos*** requires an ultimate and *tacitly profound* creative *maintenance* by a *super*sensible yet artfully, "*Un*knowing" *Player* participant!

---

*See Sub-Rational Synonyms (selected list) (Page 103) and the discussion of how this mechanism acts to rationalize and perpetuate aberrant behavior and belief.
**See Appendix III for the Kosmic Equation: A primal post-traumatic identification or indistinction between the 6th and 7th domains both characterizes and enables all human aberration. The Holon submerged in and "dominated" by pain-enforced memorialization and belief is actually fulfilling a primal dedication to preserving the actual Kosmic pattern of existence. As an enduring and distracting paradox the sub-rational mind is a falsely valued mockery of that transcendental obligation.

The eternal objects are the pure potentials of the universe.
Actual entities differ in their realization of this potential.
A.N. Whitehead, Philosopher

Index of Appendices

I	Truth Functions	112
II	Consciousness as a Scale of Knowing	113
III	Kosmic Equation	114
IV	Cognitive Optimization Precepts	115
V	Cognitive Dialoguing Remedy	117
VI	Seminal Holosophy Canon	119
VII	Sub-Rational Indicators	121
VIII	The Physical Universe ... a Cosmic Computer?	142
IX	Holosophy Terms and Subject List	143
X	Origin of Life and Information	155
XI	Belief Frames	169
XII	Cosmic Parable	159
XIII	True "Self" Transcendence	163
XIV	Paradox as Meta-Logical Order	164
XV	The Persisting Problem as Hidden Paradox	167
XVI	Kosmic Archetypal Triads	171
XVII	Holosophy Publications	172

> "all values are graduated degrees of Quality…"
> -- Holosophy Canon

Appendix I

Hierarchy of Truth* Functions

∞ DEFINITION:	∞ COGNITIVE DESCRIPTION:	∞ UTILITY SCALE:
Transcendent Truth… Infinite but *un*specified potentiality for all as yet *un*manifest knowability and primal non-duality.	Infinite *knowability-potential for all* universal and non-duality (neither the one *nor* the many not + *or* -) not yet projected as an existence actualizing duality (+/-).	Thought as a *Potential* (non-dual) cognitive spectrum for projecting all actualizable meaning, order and value
Cognitive Truth… *Selective* knowability of *innate* hierarchic degrees and levels of implicit meaning, order and *value*	Specifically known but as yet unmanifest, or projected as actual, real, or consensualy reified as game-conditionality	Thought as yet unprojected or managed knowables, provides potentially *useful* logical order and value gradients for play
Coherent Truth… *Knowing* projected as *logically consistent* propositions or *any* represented *conceptuality*, e.g. ('unicorns have horns') or ('all crows are black')	Manifestly known but *self-generated* (actual) projection of combined conceptuality as *arbitrarily representable* knowing	Thought selectively realized as essentially *self*-endowed and projected logical order as symbolic knowables e.g.(poetry)
Consensual Truth… Knowing *objectified* as concerted, mutually combined, and shareable consensus conceptuality	Mutually comprehensible (realized) agreements between multiple viewpoints consensually made manifest	Thought used as the projected agreements and boundaries necessary for Kosmic game-playing and *gradient* value Revelation
Correspondent Truth… Symbolically descriptive propositions that attempt to convey and share discrete co-realized empirical particulars, e.g. ('that car is blue')	Ideal one to one corrospondence of a symbolic reference to a mutually observable and usefully sharable recreational Kosmos	Thought benevolently displayed to enable communication, interactive value perception, and game/domain exchange and participation
Pragmatic Truth… Higher order truths responsibly employed as means to achieve practical solutions for incremental betterment day to day	Degrees of truth value determine the workability of data-use in objective problem solving on *Domains I-VI*	Thought as reasoning capacity in using and *restoring* the calculus of betterment to discern and enhance Kosmic play
Perceptual Truth… Truth as a primary *creative act* of accurate and immediate sensory representation of an 'external' reality	The immediate consensual re-creation of a *co-experienced* external reality using healthy organs of perception	Thought as the primary perceptual apparatus that *limits perception* to actionable, game enabling and sustaining barriers
0	0	0

*Holosophy defines thought as *projected knowing* with graduated degrees of reification and habituation and *describes* "Truth" basically as a cognitive hierarchy of *symbolic and transformative* perspectives, *representing* and *accessing* a full descriptive scale of the *total capacity to Know*. Ranging from the immediacy of raw perception, up through symbolic representation and its formal logical order, to ultimate *reminding* access of the primal non-material Forms of the ultimate *patterned potentiality* for Existence, e.g. both as *cognitive* Universals ('Beauty') *and/or* specified particulars (Mozart's 'Requiem'). Truth as *value* is the cognitive framing or motivating ideal for *optimal use* of perception and ideation. It is in this higher sense that a great work of art has truth or quantitative *value* as a reminding reflection of a higher cognitive *order*, a realm of transcendence to which all *value* of symbol, object or act, gives revelatory access. Values as degrees of objective and *ascending* qualities which are the attributes of *worth* on a gradient scale of valued things, a staircase to a sublime, qualitative essence.

Holosophy and applied as a graduated cognitive "vehicle" to provide graduated access to ultimate truth-value, is as follows:

I. **Epistemological Order:** Conceptuality as cognitive potentiality for *all* meaningful order, value and actualization.
II. **Ontological Order:** Capacity to specify meaning as realized being inherent in and derived from acts of knowing.
III. **Teleological Order:** Innate reconciled duality, devolving to the manifest duality of consensually realized cyclical action and purpose (see below).
IV. **Paradoxical Order:** Concealed, but potentially manifest, meaning and order. A paradox is a seeming contradiction, a statement that is at once, presented in a physical universe (6th domain) context, as a substantive fact, but, at the same time, covertly references a hidden *non-material* meaning (7th domain). This is done without making a true distinction between the two different, irrationally superimposed, but unequal universal frames of reference! Combining the two without *domain distinction* is the source of the paradox, e.g.; *I* am lying…or "this" statement is false…or…Does the barber who only shaves those who don't shave themselves…*shave himself?* Or, people who are tolerant reject intolerance therefore are *themselves intolerant* of intolerance…a "true" but conflicted "self"-referencing duality. Similarly, unwanted conditioning (fixed ideas, conflicting intentions, with resulting mental tensions and dilemmas) result from this seemingly paradoxical equivalence and post traumatic *indistinction* between 7th domain conceptuality and 6th domain physicality…between meaning and referent, and/or between an imposed *post-traumatic memory* and an undistorted statement of fact. A targeted realization, in dialogue, is the distinction, and erasure, of the aberrant traumatically produced identification of both then and now, of thing and idea… The illogic of domain indistinction is an imposed, false 6th domain *copy* of the ultimately reconciled "non-duality" of the 8th domain.
V. **Meta-Logical Order:** Logic itself doesn't *explain* logic. Only an external ultimately higher cognitive capacity which itself is the *source* of logic, provides the transcendent Kosmic conceptuality that is senior to, and resolves, with *knowing* restored any apparent contradiction or *illogic*. For instance the philosophic tradition of "sufficient reason" (everything has a prior cause) is sanctioned by the binding logic *of the Cosmos*, however, its rigor does not apply to the 7th and 8th Kosmic domains wherein *anything* can be or not be, *for* any reason, in any time frame, or chosen locational perspective. A necessarily pre-cosmic potentiality for the specified agreements is required for the *consensual perceptual* complicity of the holon-players in the Kosmic game. Thus the innate unconstructed meta-logic of non-duality (7th domain) is cognitively projected (6th domain) as the *substantive* logic of duality i.e. something (+) enabled and actualized by the necessary and simultaneously dual, cognitive negation (-) or selective *absence of all else*, producing an enduring fabric of duality, novelty, and *play* – the Kosmos!

Appendix II   *Specified knowing is a subtraction from infinite knowability.*
                                                            -Holosophy Maxim

Consciousness as a
Hierarchic Scale of Knowing*

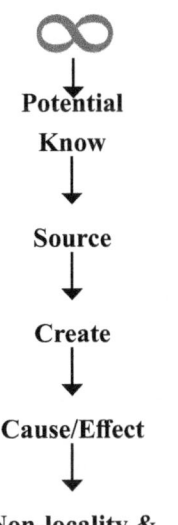

∞
↓
Potential = Infinite unspecified *Potential* for all projected knowingness enabled below as variably displayed meaning and its projectable being (elements of knowing combined)

Know
↓ = Innate conceptuality or *specified* knowables, i.e., *subtracted* primal agency conceptuality from the infinite totality of potential knowability

Source
↓ = Innate conceptual and categorical templates for specified meaning as potentially manifest existential referents, or *possibles* (*combinable* knowables)

Create
↓ = Emergent Novelty: existential forms of being (as *combined* knowability) projected as new recreational actualities (manifest forms, events or *possible* occasions)

Cause/Effect
↓ = Apparent spatio-temporal ordering of projected and manifest being as agree upon reality (existential process as volitionally coordinated *combined* knowings)

**Non-locality &
Cosmic Remnant
Entanglement** = Cosmic background wave-potentia as the remnant quantum levels underlying all physical *possibilities*, contingency, or eventuality (selectively varied probability). Background is finally reified statistically, as the co-perceived projection of *residual* Life-Game conditions and potentials.

---

* This scale represents a declining ladder or range of knowing from infinite potential at the top, down through degrees of necessary unknowing or *selective* unawareness necessary for enthralled game-endowment.

Appendix III

Kosmic Equation

> "Meaning is the specified being of knowing..."
> — Holosophic Maxim
>
> "The universe is a great dream, dreamed as one entity... the will to live... but in such a way that all its persons dream it together..."
> — Arthur Shopenhauer, Philosopher

A woodcut attributed to C. Flammarion (1842-1925) showing a medieval searcher breaking through the world's natural boundaries to see all the transcending mechanisms that create existence. (equation added...)

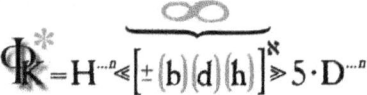

The holographic Kosmic "equation," or "optimizing algorithm," above is intended as a symbolic representation of the complete and actual Kosmic pattern of existence... Where $\Phi\!K$ is considered the divinely proportionate (and personified) matrix of all eight Kosmic domains*... which then equals infinite potentiality ∞ (eighth domain) bracketed below from which are derived its emergent aspects. First in rank, is the conceptual potentialities for intentionally manifesting the innate archetypal category themes of the primal game template: being, doing, having (7th domain). This then selectively brings about the necessary emergent ordering of the other domains beginning with the holon (H^+), the individuality or player consciousness which provides the active agency and window of participancy (1st domain) necessary to *specify* and experience the remaining five domains (5·D). These comprise the interactive fields of life and existence that Consciousness-at-large (7th and 8th D) imposes on the physical universe (6th D) as the Kosmic Life Games Playing Field.

$\aleph$ = a specifiable and derived infinity of potentials... also implying the "collapse" of an infinite possibility into a *selected* actuality

Φ = divine proportion; contains interacting hierarchic symmetries and order of the Kosmic domain template, including *personification*

[= contains the category matrix of of the primal domain elements

(= contains distinct conceptual potential for each of the catergory meaning domain sources

$\leqslant$ = source of, and of greater magnitude than

$...n$ = volitionally imposed limit to actualize each infinite possibility

Archetype = a priori (conceptual) *source* of symbolization, sometimes refers to (and is confused with) the primary representation, combined conceptuality or symbol itself.

* It is the redundant or "shadow *copy*" of the authentic, *primal* Kosmic template, that, unknowingly endowed and confused with that actual pattern provides the origin and command value of the sub-rational mind with its false game limitations and irrational fixed belief system

** Kosmic: An ancient Greek term used by Pythagoras and borrowed by Holosophy to refer to the entire universe in all its multi-dimentionality, i.e. Spiritual, mental, emotional and physical... and contrasted with "Cosmos" in its modern usage which refers only to the physical realm.

***Domain: each of the 8 primary interactive meaning-spheres of Kosmic existence... in the form of which the Life Game Themes playfully emerge and inter-act... self, family, community, humanity, all life forms, the physical universe, (plus) Conceptuality and Infinite Potential.

---

* $\Phi\!K$ is a symbolic combination of Φ as divine proportion and K representing the existence of the Kosmos in entirety.

Appendix IV

Cognitive Optimization Precepts

1. Sub-rational thinking consists of the memorial image-making of the past ... as distinct from conceptual or imaginal thought, which is immediate, evanescent cognitive novelty, and the instantaneous emergence of the actual ... sub-rationality cloaks the resulting rational choice-making, which actualizes and optimally gives value to Kosmic play.

2. The goal in life is to "think" conceptually or imaginally (without persisting mental images, 'mass' or tension) ... this enables optimized domain choice-making and value discernment, as a kosmic player.

3. The optimization calculus consists of discerning enactment of the maximum quality of existence for the maximum number of kosmic domains ... where quality could be defined as the maximum momentarily enacted valuation of Truth, Goodness, and Beauty.

4. Domain differentiation by conceptual distinction reveals any mis-assignment of domain category integrity and *re*-stores the game-enabling domain distinctions that permits optimized exchanges between them.

5. The primary basis for all aberrant domain-identity confusion is a primal stress-based but volitional mis-definition and displacement of each domain's conceptual integrity and therefore it prevents optimal interactivity.

6. The primary sub-rational basic on all domain-distinction confusions is a primal traumatic deception-based mis-definition, which is then endowed with false redundant post-traumatic meaning and continuity.

7. Ideally, the holon creates, projects, and endows momentarily relevant thoughts and *imaginal** images while not *being* or self-identifying *with* those thoughts.

8. All sub-rationality has to do with misplaced omitted, or uncertain domain categoricality, which also distorts judgment and choice.

9. Proper domain identity-recognition and endowment re-enables and re-vitalizes the actual pattern of Kosmic existence.

10. The authentic character of the holon is shaped by the capacity for creating individually optimized exchangeable items and their *value*-related domain placement.

11. All Kosmic existents are ultimately *subjects* not objects.

12. All concepts and their derived words can apply to and within all domains, modified *rationally* by individual perspective and situation, and, *sub*-rationally by fixed trauma-based, and meaning distorting, *belief* systems.

13. *Rational* choice is the innate capacity for knowing, choiceful, optimization, i.e., deciding the greater good based on actual perception and comparative evaluation of the greatest possible domain applicability with perception of each domain *-interactive* priority, relevance and exchangeable content.

14. Mis-definition and/or misplacement of an item or reference within the wrong domain is a primary sub-rational indicator ... if an element is so placed or mis-defined, it prevents that domain rational identification, valuation and game-exchangeability.

---

*Momentary, nonsubstantive image-content or persistence. Controlled visualization useful in constructive or artistic endeavors, but *not* sub-rationally fixed or persisting.

Appendix V

Cognitive Dialoguing Remedy for Sub-rational "Problems"
(Handled via Repetitive Communication Cycle to Cognitive Closure)

DEFINITIONS
a) Subjective Problem: Any persisting unwanted condition or conflicted situation that one has fixed attention on, and "can't," resolve but which also stressfully demands solution. It contains hidden balanced intentions underlying and causing persistence of "present" unwanted pictured insolubility
b) Objective Problem: How or whether to, take incremental action steps to correct an actual present or future departure from an ideal scene ... (conceptual not continually mentally pictured).
c) Condition: State of being: the actual and existing nature of something.
d) Intention: Personal volition, impulse, goal, purpose ("to ____"; to not ____"), directed focus to act or refrain from acting.
e) Novelty: A new and imaginally created unit of space and time, not based on a mentally-pictured past, but with the cognitive familiarity of direct and un-mediated knowing.

PROCEDURE: Define and assure client understanding of dialogue questions fully. Use only those questions that seem problem-relevant and interesting to client. Continue repetitive dialogue (locate earlier and similar content as necessary) and continue to cognitive closure with, restored good indicators and ultimately subjective, "problem" vanishment[*].

1. Is there a problem in the present that concerns you? Tell me about it ....
2. Tell me about your problem with ____ what part of the problem could you confront?
3. What problem about ____ could you confront?
4. What two things about ____ can you confront?
5. Get the idea of solving a problem with ____? (Not solving)

[*]Erasure of the "problem" by *volitional cessation* of its continuous redundant mental image creation of fixed and false opponency.

6. Give me some answers concerning ____ (solutions for ____)
7. Tell me what is unknown about the problem ...
8. Think of something you have (done/withheld) concerning the problem.
9. Tell me about the problem with ____. What part of that problem could you be responsible for?
10. What action of yours has another been responsible for?
11. Think of a problem of comparable importance to that problem.
12. Who or what has influenced you regarding the problem/issue?
13. Is there an earlier confusion or stress similar to the current problem?
14. What part of the problem haven't you been able to influence/change?
15. Is the problem happening in this moment? ... Locate it ... point to it.
16. Where exactly is the problem?
17. Take a careful look and see if there is anything you could be contributing to the persisting problem/condition ... e.g., a hidden belief, unchanging idea, assumption.

REMEDIAL QUERIES:
18. Does the problem have parts? Describe them distinctly.
19. Could some part of the problem be seen as valuable in some way?
20. Is "it" still the same problem? What isn't changing about the problem?
21. Mistaking a condition for a problem? Re-define difference.
22. Mistaking a condition for an intention. Re-define difference.
23. Is there a hidden and/or earlier counter-intention ("to" or "to not" ____!) in the problem?
24. False balance or seeming equivalence of intentions still in the problem? Some intention not yours?
25. Problem seems unsolvable, but also urgently demands a solution?
26. Hidden harmful or unethical purpose underlying the problem?
27. Earlier confusion related to the problem?
28. New problem not yet stated or problem changing ... something else wrong. How is it now?

Appendix VI

The basic conundrums of life result from confusing semantics (meaning) with syntax (language structure*).*
Holosophy Canon

Seminal Holosophy Canon

A Reality is an agreement in progress ... so is a game.
A Reality requires observer-participation ... so does a game.
A Reality has variable options and barriers ... so has a game.
A Reality can be won or lost .. or transcended ... so can a game.
A Reality contains arbitrary rules or "laws" ... so does a game.
A Reality is not internally complete and consistent ... neither is a game.
A Reality requires time, place, form and event ... so does a game.
A Reality is not self-generated .. .neither is a game.
In a game the players can decide to resume play after an interruption ... ?
...Does Reality include a re-incarnate resumption of Play?

Any true metaphysic of consciousness must address three fundamental problems:

I. The "basis" Problem...

Why is it that we experience a mere "sentient slice" of the-vast universe around us ... why does awareness have a private and separate perimeter if that defining (and excluding) perimeter *is itself*... an undistinguished material part of an endlessly interconnected and "smeared out" cosmic quantum background?
...How are these quantum "dots" connected within a particular perspective and what *connects* them *purposively* ... to "form" the qualia and gestalts of ordinary experience?

II. The "binding" problem...

How can the putative "neural correlates" of consciousness be *bound together* to provide both a unity of awareness (personal agency) *and* unitized objects of perception (gestalts or *qualia*) which have *holistic* features seemingly different in kind from mere collections of discrete and *material* brain states or wave frequencies? Can such a *process* be conscious due to the number and mere interconnectivity of its *physical parts*, however vast? What *connects* the dots to form an image... more dots?

III. The "bestowing" problem ...

Are holons "condemned" to be free? How can a personal existence itself, including freedom of choice and responsibility, be arbitrarily and individually bestowed by a diety, *however* benevolent, *without a prior existential capacity, of each recipient,* to accept or reject such a demanding *imposition* of a "Self-creationed" volition *and* determination? Can freedom be arbitrarily *bestowed as a compulsion,* and *then* punished for an ensuing flawed exercise? Or does each holon have the original and innate self-generative capacity logically necessary for *actual* free choice, but somehow, *also rationally consistent** with the infinitely potential "endowing" capacity of an all powerful, all knowing, *and benevolent* Deity (8th domain).

---

*True rationality derives from and is freely consistent with *some* ultimate objective, and *consensual* source and standard. Can agency *and* rationality be truly *bestowed* without the "consent of the governed"?

Appendix VII

Sub-Rational Indicators: A General List of Unwanted (Sub-Optimal) Conditions

The sub-rational indicators are a compendium of the character, emotional and attitudinal traits symptomatic of sub-rationality which we have observed over the years to fall* away *when addressed* in the course of the Holosophy Counseling Programs, and which have been arranged and codified in the categories, and with the specific characteristics provided below. While not necessarily exhaustive, they are a good cross section of the observable range of sub-rational experience, and will more than sufficient to assess, plan and customize the identification, examination and erasure through dialogue of specified unwanted and sub-volitional behavior. The client should, however, feel free to expand the list based on personal experience. Increasing familiarity with the list will better enable him to do so ...

The sub-rational indicators below comprise over 150 typically redundant and sub-optimum (i.e., destructive, contra-survival) post-traumatic mental and emotional states and conditions which though comprehensive are not complete ... These have been defined, codified, and arranged alphabetically into eight general sub-rational categories: Mal-Emotion; Criticalness; Continuity; Dis-Interest; Confusion; Dis-Ability; Generality; and Mis-Perception.

---

*These categories convey (based on long term observation) types of specific unwanted conditions that are extinguished or "un-created" when fully inspected during dialogue. We suggest that the sub-optimum psychological conditions which improve or *erase* during their address in counseling are also sub-*rational* to begin with. Their erasure restores the eclipsed optimum and rationally natural state. Remember that list is a helpful but *limited*, 'solo' application. Some indicators require deeper viewing and access more proper to a counselor or an assisted Cognitive-Optimization program.

I. MAL-EMOTION

Definition: an irrational, ineffective and unpleasant emotional reaction; ingrained uncontrolled negative emotion, usually irrelevant to the actual experience of the moment and continuing long past the circumstance or event assumed to be its cause, and experienced with an often compulsive urgency and seeming lack of volition.

Alienation: withdrawing or distancing oneself from things, persons, or former attachments; self-exile or "lonerism," often tinged with self-pity, "woundedness," "numbness," or steely resolve to be invulnerable to the "pain" of *any* disappointment or betrayal.

Anger: physically aggressive feeling of displeasure, antagonism or hostility toward another person or thing with characteristic and stressful dysfunction.

Anxiety: a painful or apprehensive uneasiness of mind, usually over an irrationally anticipated or impending ill; fearful concern or interest; self-doubt about one's capacity to cope with a fancied adversity.

Apathy: dispirited lack of any appropriate feeling, emotion, caring or concern.

Boredom: an unpleasant state of being irresponsibly devoid of interest or purpose.

Carefulness: marked by excessive concern or solicitude, by extreme caution, wariness, or prudence, or by an overly painstaking effort to avoid errors or omissions.

Covert Hostility: secret enmity or hidden unfriendliness, injuriousness or ill-will; antagonism, opposition or resistance in thought and/or action accompanied by pretended liking.

Degradation: a shameful or humiliating sense of diminished or lost status, rank or worth.

Envy: a painful or resentful awareness of an advantage or possession seemingly or actually enjoyed by another often joined with a compulsive desire to exclusively possess the same advantage or possession.

Fear: a strong sense of dread, alarm or panic generally accompanying an anticipation or fixed awareness of danger whether real or imagined.

Grief: a sense of deep, enduring and poignant distress often accompanying, extending and recurring beyond an apparent or actual loss, e.g., of a loved one or a valued object or condition.

Guilt: an oppressive sense that one has solely caused, and is "to blame" for, the suffering or condition of another; obsessive, regretful "self" -condemnation ...

Handle It Myself: a conviction, decision or resolve, tinged with covert anger or resentment that one must handle something oneself if it is to be "done right" or done at all.

Hate: extreme aversion, dislike, or enduring and active enmity or hostility toward something.

Hopelessness: a state of having no expectation of ultimate good or success; of not being susceptible to remedy or cure; of being incapable of solution, management or accomplishment. Impatience: restlessness; extreme limited sufferance; shortness of temper, especially under stress, delay, opposition, or challenge.

Jealousy: excessive or victimized intolerance of rivalry or unfaithfulness; apprehensiveness of the loss of another's exclusive devotion; hostility toward a rival or another believed to enjoy a valued advantage regarding a situation, object or person, "rightfully" one's own.

Loss: a continuing sense of emotional harm, deprivation or desolation accompanying and persisting beyond a removal, absence or separation from something or someone of value.

Malaise: a vague sense of unease often associated with the onset of an illness, or impending loss or dissatisfaction.

Manic: excessively or unreasonably enthusiastic; irrelevantly hyperactive or loquacious; gleefulness'.

Misery: a continuous unhappy or emotionally distressing state of suffering and want, usually accompanied by an apparent deprivation or persisting affliction of some kind.

Nervousness: negative excitation; jumpiness, fidgetiness or oversensitivity accompanied by tense concern over a possible challenge, unwanted result, or possibility.

Outrage: being "poised" for a victimized sense of injustice and aggressive susceptibility to being 'offended'; aggrieved, or disappointed.

Persisting Upset: a state of being mentally or emotionally troubled which continues or endures long after the act or event, which seemed to have caused it has passed.

Revulsion: a strong, often violent or "sickening" sense of being repelled, usually by something automatically deemed repugnant, offensive or evil.

Righteous Indignation: a "lofty" sense of moral up-rightness accompanied by a "justifiable" outrage against the supposed offending party or circumstance.

Sadness: a persisting, emotionally painful, poignant or "bittersweet" feeling often associated with a sense of irretrievable loss of some kind, or an event or circumstance automatically thought to be "a tragedy" or "a shame," such as an untimely death.

Sense of Failure: defeatedness; a deflating sense that one is congenitally unable to be successful, achieve goals or perform effectively the routine responses to challenge or functions of living.

Shame: a sense of self-abnegating guilt, shortcoming or social impropriety, or of humiliating disgrace or embarrassing disrepute or admonition.

Stubborn: intractable; unmanageable; obsessive unwillingness to deviate from a fixed pattern; heedless of suggestion.

Suspicion: the act of critically suspecting that something is wrong or amiss without proof, or on insufficient evidence.

Sympathy: commiserating with and therefore validating another's victimization; an automatic, often deemed virtuous or even morally obligatory, habitual co-experiencing or sharing of another's suffering, sadness or grief; co-suffering, as contrasted with empathy or compassion, based on the assumption that self-reduction is required to help or communicate to a suffering or disadvantaged person ... 'feeling their pain'.

"Tolerance": exhibiting strained forbearance, endurance or "putting up with" often under hidden protest.

Unhappy: typically not cheerful or glad; habitually causing or "subject to" misfortune; without a sense of purpose, participation, productivity or fulfillment in life.

Worry: mental distress or agitation resulting from exaggerated concern, usually for something impending or anticipated; obsessively visualized threat, menace or negative consequence.

II. CRITICALNESS

Definition: an obsessive, unreasoned and hostile devaluation of persons or things; the habitual, often rationalized minimizing, attacking or negative distortion of any actual value or worth, which masks the deeper, sub-rational intention to destroy or remove by force, anything that "shouldn't be" in the moment when it actually is ...

Abandonment: critical departure from or isolation of a blamed person or situation usually to covertly punish.

Argumentative: obsessive election of opponency; unproductive conflict; habitual protest or "againstness" based on hidden destructive need.

Asserted Rightness: compulsively and insistently positing the "validity" or superiority of one's viewpoint, position or actions; needing to assert one's "rightness" with the implied wrongness of another; a fixed "knowing best."

Belittling: making less, little or nothing of others; compulsively including deprecating or critical comments in one's demeaning appraisal of another.

Blaming: denial of any personal responsibility while mal-emotionally attributing injurious, censorious or "bad" cause or agency to others; holding others solely and punitively responsible for one's (or any) unwanted condition.

Contemptuousness: diminishing criticalness or hostility toward those (including self) seemingly incapable of, or inherently deficient in exercising a desired degree of intelligence, skill, judgment, expertise, etc.

Defensive: self-justifying; protectively explaining or rationalizing one's behavior or actions in an effort to diminish an apparent threat and prove self right (or not wrong) and others wrong (or not right.)

Disapproval: judging to be unworthy, immoral, unacceptable or wrong.

"Don't Need Help": a conviction, usually tinged with defiance, stubbornness, or denial that some real and possible assistance is unneeded; or that one can do alone that which might actually requires cooperation or assistance.

Gossip: the often gleeful or titillating spreading of rumors or reports of an intimate, salacious, sensational, malicious or privileged nature which, by virtue of its harmfulness or demeaningness, actually represents an indirect criticalness toward, or attack on another or others.

Grudging: giving or allowing unwillingly or reluctantly; ambivalent or resentful compliance or acknowledgment.

Hidden Standard: all or nothing thinking; which doesn't allow gradient, requiring of oneself or others a higher level of understanding, achievement, expertise or accomplishment without allowing for intermediate steps or gains; habitually minimizing progress by negating any step toward the goal because it is not the "final" attainment; "everything or *nothing*," a persisting sub-rational and losing comparison.

Hostile Individuation: excessive, often arrogant sense of separateness from rational participation in a group often following harmful acts against that group and usually based on a hidden need to protect the group from one's continuing harmful intention; compulsive abandonment of allegiance accompanied by a false devaluation of the group or individual abandoned to obviate the harm caused.

Ignobleness: characterized by baseness or meanness of spirit.

Invalidating: weakening, making little or less of; destroying the truth, legitimacy or worth of something, often to explain earlier offenses against that thing.

Making Wrong: a compulsive proving or showing of another's convictions or actions to be wrong, unjust or unreasonable, often by a contrived victimization of self by the other.

Martyrdom: a sense of suffering "willingly but undeservedly" for some cause or person, allegedly for the sake of one's principles; covertly self-interested suffering.

Mis-emotional Evaluation: a decision, conclusion, judgment or assessment tinged with or stemming from negative emotion such as anger, resentment or jealousy.

No Trust: a belief or attitude that the character, ability, strength or truth of other people or things can "never" be relied upon.

No Remedy: the irrationally self-serving conviction, often militantly and aggressively asserted, that help or any degree of betterment is impossible, non-existent or harmfully intended.

Protesting: ineffective and contentious complaining, objecting, actively resisting or displaying unwillingness, usually to an idea or course of action.

Reductionism: the tendency to reduce complex data or phenomena perceived as hostile to one's fixed ideas to simplistic, less significant or 'nothing but' causal terms; devaluation by habitual, usually materialistic, interpretation which omits vital data, context, consciousness, or other aspects of total existence from consideration as to cause or source.

Regret: persisting grief or pain, tinged with mal-emotions such as disappointment, longing or remorse, over some past event, action or occurrence; the irrational, often debilitating longing for the reversal or cancellation of past events or misfortune.

Revenge: self-justified retaliation against the source of a real or imagined insult or injury.

Self-Critical: disparaging of self; considering self to be intrinsically flawed or unacceptable; self-compulsive effacement.

Suspicious: premature, and often undeserved assignment of wrongness, potential enmity or harmful purpose.

Tense Denial: a negating or protesting of something, usually the-assertion or accusation of another, accompanied by nervousness or stress, or the feeling of being undeservedly attacked.

Too Intense: overly serious; morose; preoccupied to the point of tense and persisting urgency or distraction.

Unforgiving: unable to give up a persisting bitterness or resentment of, or claim to requital for, a past "victimization" by a person or event.

Victimization: unadmittedly failing to assume responsibility for one's own condition; resentfully attributing one's failure, injury or unwanted condition wholly to others; dishonest "suffering," or confusion.

III. CONTINUITY

Definition: the apparency of sameness or unchangingness; of seamlessness or on-going, effect contrasted with the actual discontinuous and novel seriality of each differentiated and unique "moment-to-moment" interval of experience.

Excessive 'Need' To: an overly pronounced sense of obligation, requirement or pressure to be, do or have something.

Fanatic: marked by excessive and irrational zeal and often intense, belligerent and uncritical devotion to (or opposition to) a belief or opinion.

Fixed Attention: inability to shift one's attention from one thing to another at will; a compulsive focusing on or returning to something; obsessive introversion or extroversion; mental 'stuckness'.

Habit or Addictive Behavior: automatically repetitive or compulsive indulgence in or abstinence from something, such as alcoholic drinking, promiscuity, compulsive gambling, overeating, smoking or any obsessive activity.

Looking That Doesn't Change a Mental State: inspection of a sub-rational indicator which does not result in alleviating or dissolving it because of an interjected but unnoticed "slant," hidden perspective or standard preventing direct observation and therefore honest communication and erasure. "I see it...but it doesn't change."

Misplaced Concreteness: attributing solidity or dense unchangeability to that which is persisting but purely conceptual or symbolic, such as "hopelessness" or "no money."

Perceives "Factoid" in Place of Fact: perceives or accepts as objective fact an observation which is actually overlaid and distorted by subjective opinion, supposition or conjecture.

Persisting Unwanted Condition or "Stuck Picturing": an undesired state of mind, set of mental images, conditions, or preoccupation, which seems to continue despite one's desire to be rid of it.

Procrastination: unreasonable neglect, or postponing attending to something, usually accompanied by a rationalized negative attitude, dread or aversion projected onto the omitted obligation, whether noticed or unnoticed.

Self Consciousness: undue preoccupation with the impression one is making upon others; overconcern with obtaining approval or reassurance; morbid and sustained introspection.

Subjective Problem: internal mental conflict or picturing, projected outward and seen as an unwanted and seemingly "unresolvable" or unchangeable external condition which also demands solution; an attitudinal "can't" or specious personal disempowerment.

Uncaused/**Uncreated**: 'menacing otherness': feeling as if one is a "victim" of an overwhelming and uncaused existence or presence; a sense of being at the personally uncaused menacing effect of someone or something over which one has no ownership, authorship or control.

"Worn Outness": feeling emotionally or psychologically thwarted or beaten by life, either in general or by a convincing set of too "real" circumstances, events or onuses that have 'obstructed' one's aspirations.

IV. DIS-INTEREST

Definition: Covertly suppressed or misplaced interest in an area of life, where such interest and its resulting contact, confronting and interaction would reveal and eventually erase a sub-rational "protective" commitment to valuable fixed or habitual ideas, attitudes or disabled behavior about that part of life.

Arrogance: actively diminishing the value of others while asserting and exaggerating one's own.

Can't or Must Create Interest: an inability to find value in something actually worthwhile, or a sense that one should find value in or interact with someone or something, arising from fixed notions about the absence or presence of value or worth.

Can't Remember: apparently unable (or convinced that it is impossible) to recall something; feeling blocked, fogged in or continuously blank about some past thing; sub-volitionally selective unawareness of the past.

Complacency: lackadaisical or incurious self-satisfaction usually accompanied by habitual unawareness of any actual dangers, deficiencies or need for betterment.

Contactlessness: obsessive disconnectedness; a sense of not touching or being a part of anything; alienation; enforced remoteness or dissociation.

Distracted by Lesser Priorities: an automatic drifting of attention or consciousness away from important or priority matters onto less important or trifling matters.

Elsewhereness: not being present in the moment; automatically or unconsciously dwelling on the past, or daydreaming ineffectively about the future; thinking of other things distractedly, rather than with the attentiveness the present moment demands.

Emotionless: deadness, numbness; feeling "no feelings"; passive insensitivity.

Facetious: jocularity or levity in an often clumsy or inappropriate manner to mask hidden misemotion or intent.

'Got it made': a sense of exaggerated confidence or fixed self-assurance, usually tinged with arrogance or complacency, which ignores the big picture or larger issue of sustaining and increasing betterment, and instead clinging to a rationalized and unchanging "positive" self-image.

Humorlessness: "deadpanish"; literalness: seeing no humor or lightness in anything; focused solely on the "serious" side of life; inability to get distance from, or "lighten" an experience.

Ignoring 'Small' Awarenesses of Causation: not noticing or "listening" to one's subtle intimations; discounting discernment, promptings or intuitions of possible incremental betterment and change; 'always knew' any realization resulting from a dialogue ...

Laxity: undutiful neglectence, or omission of discipline, resolve or intent necessary to accomplish a rational task or result.

"No Sympathy": a harsh, cold or defensively indifferent attitude toward another's suffering, as opposed to a position of being neither sympathetic nor unsympathetic but compassionate (a distanced but rationally caring and active benevolence.)

Non-Participation: fixed avoidance of joining in; typically abstaining from group efforts or alliances; acting the "loner."

Not Confronting known and actual importances: ignoring the obvious; "backing off or resisting facing and handling difficult but important issues, people or events, present or past.

Not Enough Time: an enervating sense that sufficient 'time' does not exist to accomplish something, as opposed to knowingly prioritizing and apportioning time as a controllable resource for accomplishment.

Remote: cut off from, distant; unattached to; obsessively disconnected.

Same Realization Over and Over: a repetitive "knowing," awareness or insight which is not applied, or does not result in change of condition or deepen or expand in time; habitual adherence to an unchanging philosophical core belief or ineffective "common sense" conviction or "fixed idea."

Stuck in an Accomplishment or Win: resting on one's laurels or living in the past; dwelling on or continuously returning to a past achievement, without adding to one's store of progressively evolving accomplishments and wisdom.

Uninteresting Object or Person: considering a person or thing to be intrinsically "uninteresting" or without merit, as opposed to recognizing one's capacity to generate interest or choose to withhold interest or selectively intend interest to accommodate ethical goals or projects.

Unwilling to Apply Ethics: willfully ignoring what would be best for the greatest number effected and instead choosing to act with a narrow and perverse focus of interest, negating the wider rational balance of concerns which achieve the greater good for all domains.

V. CONFUSION

Definition: a persisting seemingly 'honest' failure to comprehend, a convincingly oppressive mental disorganization of thought process and attention, which actually overlays a sub-volitionally selected and fixed balance of opposing convictions regarding a resisted or desired subject, situation or person.

Blankness: persisting dull-headedness; mentally "frozen" or stubbornly numb; seemingly unable to think, imagine, or recall.

Can't Assign Correct Importances: calculated inability to prioritize or evaluate the worth or importance of some things in relation to others in order to prevent realization decision or planned achievement.

Conflicting "Truths": inability to establish shades of difference between opposing ideas or issues, which appear to be equally real, true or factual resulting in a self-serving impairment of action or judgment.

Convinced after Impact or Duress: "brainwashed"; having the "truth" stressfully; enforced, delusional believing or adamant conviction after suffering stress, pain or punishment to "correct" or "reform" a previous state of non-believing; "post-traumatic;" or post-hypnotic suggestion.

Dogged Assertion of Conviction: a compulsive or stubborn adherence to a false belief despite _established contrary evidence, observation, or reasonable argument and discourse.

Dopey: semi-comatose; an enduring state of mental sluggishness, thickness, dullness, stupidity.

Insolubility: the apparency that a particular problem or condition cannot be resolved or changed no matter what effort is applied to it; a hopeless and menacing dilemma which yet demands a solution and fixes attention.

No or Slow Cognitions: failure to have normal insights or realizations when new, and particularly profound material, is presented to one; selective incomprehension in the service of a fixed pattern of avoidance or sub-rational preservation.

Persisting Complexity or Mystery: failure to grasp the meaning of something despite repeated and varied exposition; selective unawareness of the larger, rational context which, when understood, erases the narrower, fixed context of an apparent insolubility formed in the past and misplaced in the present.

Robotic: automatic, machine-like; going through motions; falling into habit, repetition or echoing rather than bringing fresh awareness and intent to something; irresponsibly following orders or assigning external cause for one's actions; mindless reenactment.

Slow or Unstable Learning: sluggish or resistive grasp of new information, often characterized by lapses, setbacks or forgetting; "stupidity;" sub-volitionally patterned mental resistance.

Sudden Tiredness: "feelings" of fatigue brought on "mysteriously," or by enervating negative "feelings" or "thoughts" rather than by physical exertion or strenuous effort.

Trouble with Concepts, Words, and Study: a persistent resistance to the learning of theoretical or conceptual material; a defensive "blockheadedness" or a covertly purposeful blankness with respect to such learning.

Don't Notice: obliviousness; unheeding failure to perceive one's surroundings or to note obvious importances or significant things as an insulation from the betterment derived from systematic noticing and remedial action.

Greedy: unethical desire for possession, sensation or status in excess of what is rationally necessary, appropriate or fair.

Illness/Injury Prone: tendency to frequently experience and suffer from proneness to physical ailments and accidents.

Inattentive: unwilling to concentrate or pay attention; revelation avoidance.

Incompleteness: a troubling sense that one is fundamentally flawed, or not whole or sufficient, or that something vital is missing from a product or experience.

Indecisive: wavering; unable to make decisions or choose; perpetually at "loggerheads;" submerged in a covertly self-imposed dilemma.

Intemperate: given to excessive and unthinking indulgences, particularly of appetite or passion, as in intemperate drinking or drug use.

Knowingly Dishonest: consciously and willfully misrepresenting the truth of a situation, often to justify unethical behavior.

Know it's Wrong: compulsive action desire or decision with a partial knowledge of inappropriateness that is insufficient to enable rationale restraint or control; rationalized obsessive need, greed, or infatuation.

Lacking Intention: aimlessness, purposelessness; taking no responsibility for causing harm, or failing to help, by volitional reservation of the sustained intent necessary.

Loses Gains: forgets, "unlearns," consistently reverts to previous state of lesser knowledge or ability to sabotage an ultimate or progressive revelation or rehabilitation.

Need to Please: obsessive, often obsequious unwillingness to be thought ill of or be disliked; prone to servility or propitiativeness to gain imagined favor, approval, or affection.

No Goal: having no dreams, no desires, no ambitions, no game, no purpose, no obstacles to overcome; an unwillingness to participate in and be a full player in the game of life.

Perversity: capriciousness as contrasted with spontaneity; willful rejection, corruption or abuse of a known good; intentional irrationality; arbitrary harming action despite prior agreement with norms or codes of behavior.

Procrastination: habitually avoiding the willed or volitional compliance with or completion of a task, duty or other commitment.

No Confidence: "wimpishness," low self-esteem; representing oneself to be unable or ineffectual.

Self-Sabotage: the obsessive re-enactment of a hidden scenario from the past to bring about an apparently "uncaused" failure or self-limitation in the present.

Uncommunicativeness: an irrational conviction that communication, or direct, honest confrontation, will not help, resolve or improve an unwanted condition, or achieve a wanted one.

Unfocused: "Fuzzy," indirect wavering of intention or resolve which impedes accomplishment; hesitant or scattered.

Unhandled Physical Condition: calculated neglect of or failing to attend to or remedy an illness, injury or physical deficiency, which then becomes a continuing and chronic distraction.

Unproductive: lazy; working without result; contributing little or nothing; avoiding accomplishment or real exchange.

Unwilling to Take Action: factual but irrational passivity; deleterious neglect.

Vacillating: oscillating between two positions; harmful failure to make a decision or choice; shifting compulsively between viewpoints or peaks and valleys of sub-rational emotion or intent to achieve inaction.

VII GENERALITY

Definition: a non-legitimate symbolic totality or "allness" not subject to confirming observation; non-specific; usually attributed without full contextual awareness and incorporated in a fixed, sub-rational belief system to avoid precise and direct viewing or handling of a real situation or problem, or to legitimize a reactive agenda.

All Inclusiveness: lumping a class of things together inappropriately; failing to make distinctions between separate things, even if similar ... "everybody knows."

'Always': seeing things as being invariably one way or another, failing to allow for exceptions.

Blurred Distinction: failing to make a distinction between approximately similar things; nonspecificity.

Confused Levels of Meaning or Abstraction: failing to perceive the distinctions in definition or concept with multiordinal (i.e., a full range of) meaning; confusing "map" with territory; undifferentiated nuances, no 'gray-scale'.

Category Error: sub-rational confusion or blurring of distinction between conceptual realms or domains of meaning or existence, e.g. picture/concept, holon/mind, self/image, etc.

Enforced Equivalence: tendency to insistently equate one thing with another rather than allow for the possibility of many different relationships and distinctions between them.

Everyone Knows: irresponsible, generic attribution of a particular point of knowledge to 'everyone', or a general grouping; not allowing for the possibility that some do not know or for specific origin. Use of' 'they,' referring to an unspecified grouping of others to assert, allege, prove or disguise a point.

Fixed Context: habitual viewpoint; unwillingness to consider or imagine alternative or expanded perspectives, which might positively reframe a particular experience; no awareness of broader or deeper context for a negative experience.

Fixed Definition: perceiving only one definition or meaning for a word or symbol versus recognizing and utilizing its full spectrum of applied meaning.

Illogical: falsely assuming, or denying, a relationship between concepts or things; faulty reasoning which inhibits rational choice and judgment.

Literalness: focusing on accuracy or inaccuracy of a detail as opposed to the big picture; adhering to the "letter of the law" rather than the intent of the law; context insensitivity as in lacking a sense of humor.

'Never': dismissing of all possibilities, allowing for no possibility.

Non-Multiordinality: considering a word to have a singled or fixed meaning rather than a full spectrum of meanings depending on a changing context; fixedly non-interpretive.

Unwarranted Generalizations: global assumptions or assertions which are not demonstrable or have no basis in logic or fact and which mask direct viewing or support a conviction irrationally.

VIII. MIS-PERCEPTION

Definition: the sub-aware superimposition of post-traumatic mental images from the past over the reality of present experience to bring about an unknowing and distorted perceptual conformity of the present to the dictates of a hidden traumatic past; a post-traumatic re-enactment; delusional returning to the "safety" of the past; replacing fact with "factoid," including the reimpositions of the original perceptions contained in the trauma; psychosomatic sensation.

Negative (or Positive) Coloration: the superimposition of a mental image from a past moment of pain, stress or unconsciousness which creates a delusional reframing of the actual experience of the present in terms of the earlier trauma. Something quite harmless can seem menacing: dog = bite= all dogs bite= all dogs dangerous (by irrational association.) Non-differentiation of Word and Thing: failing to distinguish between the symbolic nature of a word and the thing it represents.

"Not Invented Here" Syndrome: an unfriendliness toward things not created or approved by self or one's group.

"Too Many," "Too Much": attributing negative or disabling cause over one to an apparently excessive quantity or degree of something experienced, rather than to the present context from which a thing is controlled or used or enacted; inhibition of the capacity for self-renewal of purpose, interest, or perception; not in the (new) moment.

"Positioning": Unethical emphasis or exaggeration of the supposed "desirable" (or undesirable) qualities of a person, place, thing, event or circumstance to persuade or influence another's viewpoint or perception to accept or reject it.

Preference for "Packaged" Perceptions: Unnoticed or obsessive reliance on authority or on "pre-digested" or externally managed perception; attribution of inordinate value to rumors herd mentality, gossip, third-party perceptions, media "facts," docudramas, "sound bites," sensationalism or group biases.

Psychosomatic Sensations: superimposition on the body of past physical perceptions contained in traumatic experiences; unwanted non-relieved physical and/or emotional sensations not connected to actual physical pathology, impact or injury; tension-based sensations (such as "nervous stomach") often resulting from the stress of conflicting purposes contained in past mental pictures; "post traumatic syndrome."

Time Distortion: the oppressive sense that time is passing more quickly or slowly than it actually is, often related to a duress which activates the reactive indicator.

Selective Unawareness: unknowing but volitional unwillingness to experience; contrived obliviousness in the service of sub-volitional agendas. This may be observed in the disavowing of a previously confirmed and demonstrated certainty that a specific reactive indicator is reactive and can be erased. The indicator may occur in a new context in which it doesn't "seem" reactive, until erasure of this variant reactive indicator reveals again the pattern of covert selectivity.

Spatial Distortion: the oppressive sense of insufficient, tight or "collapsed" space (or claustrophobia), or of overabundant or unpleasantly boundless space or time; "endlessness."

Trivialization: Devaluation of important significances, values, experiences or things perceived, to eliminate them from consideration as data in a context of realization.

"Ugly/Big Nose" Syndrome: automatically misperceiving a factual irregularity as a factoid deformity; feeling a knee-jerk revulsion toward something, the action of which is supported or "justified" by commonly-held bias against or preference for that thing; a self-serving and false authentication of reactive criticalness, justified by a critical, pictured, superimposition over the actual presence of a suboptimum object or fact.

Garrulousity: empty talking; unknowing but strategic avoidance of real communication; substituting a mannerist mode of communication for authentic being and connection; hiding behind seemingly rational verbiage, or "occupying the buzzword bushes."

Malaise (see also under mal-emotion): a vague sense of dis-ease ... often associated with the onset of an illness, and is often psychosomatic.

Appendix VIII

The Physical Universe ... a Cosmic Computer Simulation? (*excerpted*)

(A popular argument for the simulation hypothesis came from University of Oxford philosopher, Nick Bostrum, in 2003, when he suggested that members of an advanced civilization with enormous computing power might decide to run simulations of their ancestors. The would probably have the ability to run many, many such simulations, to the point where the vast majority of minds would actually be artificial ones within such simulations, rather than the original ancestral minds. So simple statistics suggest it is much more likely that we are among the simulated minds.

And there are other reasons to think we might be virtual. For instance, the more we learn about the universe, the more it appears to be based on mathematical laws. Perhaps that is not a given, but a function of the nature of the universe we are living in. "If I were a character in a computer game, I would also discover eventually that the rules seemed completely rigid and mathematical," said Max Tegmark, a cosmologist at the Massachusetts Institute of Technology (MIT). "that just reflects the computer code in which it was written.")

… But of course you aren't living in a computer simulation. Here's why:

We begin with this question: What is computation? Computation is a mapping of an input to an output according to a set of rules (an algorithm). the output is a function of the input, calculated for each independent variable in the input. For example, as I type this post, the electrical signal evoked by each keystroke is mapped to a pattern of electrons on my computer screen, according to the rules of the algorithm in my Microsoft Word program.

Note that the mapping is independent of the meaning of the input and the output signals. Microsoft Word pays no heed to the meanings conveyed by my keystrokes. The program doesn't "care" anything at all. It merely maps the electrical signal generated by my keystrokes to electrical signals on my computer screen. It is the electro-mechanical process, not any kind of comprehension. Computation is mapping of signals, and pays no heed to the meaning of the signals it maps. Computation pays no heed to the meaning of anything.

Now, the next question. What is the mind? What is the human ability by which we ask the question, "Am I living in a computer simulation?" What is it about a thought that distinguishes a thought from other things, like physical objects? Nineteenth-century German philosopher Franz Brentano gave an answer that seems decisive: Thoughts are always about something, whereas physical objects are never (intrinsically) about anything. He called the aboutness of thoughts "intentionality," using a word derived from the scholastic philosophers' theory of mind that dates back to Aristotle.

Thoughts are intentional, in the sense that they always point to something—to a concept, to an object, to a person, etc. Our thoughts always mean something. Our thoughts always have an object (conceptual or physical) to which they are intrinsically directed from the scholastic philosophers' theory of mind that dates back to Aristotle...

So are we living in a computer simulation? As I noted above, meaning is precisely what computation lacks. The most fundamental human power—the power of thought to have meaning—is just what a computer simulation cannot do.

Computation is syntax, whereas thought is semantics. If we were living in a computer simulation, and our minds were computation, the one thing we couldn't do is think.

We couldn't ask the question, "Are we living in a computer simulation?" if we were living in a computer simulation, the irony here is that, of all the possible fundamental truths of reality, the notion that we are living in such a simulation is the one we can rule out simply because it's self-refuting.

If we are living in a computer simulation, we couldn't think to ask the question.

-Michael Egnor, M.D., neurosurgeon

Appendix IX

Holosophy: Terms and Subject List (Basic and Advanced)*

1. Increments of Betterment (necessary sequencing of rational choices to optimize).
2. Rational choice/greater good for all domains, qualitative survival.
3. Obsessive withholding as sub-rational concealment of discreditable acts.
4. Persisting retributive reflex/sub-rational/indicator tolerant com-cycle completion resistance to avoid erasure.
5. Holon as self-specified non-physical viewpoint, with abilities to postulate and perceive; a creative "nothingness" as distinct from a physical entity.
6. Knowledge of sub-rational emotional indicators enable useful erasure distinctions to restore rational behavior.
7. Sub-rationally experienced tone-scale as objective criteria (mal-emotion defined as boredom and below) for defining aberration.
8. Erasure/*volitional cessation of creation* of redundant mental picturing. (Giggle manifested as relief-realization of "past is present" absurdity.)
9. Com-cycle/dialogue cycle pealing the "onion" of layered untruth to reveal the concealed truth of redundant mental creation.
10. Holon/Mind/Body ... Mind versus Brain ... extended individuality ... cosmic histories (personal reality proportionate to charge-off/case).
11. Life as game analogy (actual pattern of existence) = "LILA" matrix/paradigm.

---

* These Holosophic terms and subjects are intended to be useful, conceptual, "instigators" of thoughtful and inquiring seminar discussion and as selective dialogue entry into both the basic and more advanced aspects of Holosophy and its practical applications to philosophy, life, and living.

12. Player/Pawn top-down ranking (Game Maker, Ace, Player, Pawn, Broken Piece) ... to mere spectator.
13. Consensual game participation; thralldom mutually actualized as play.
14. Scales: Be Do Have = ARC = Understanding/co-existence of timeless ultimates/non-locally projected wave-form reduction.
15. Non-material/dichotomous points of playing fields/kosmic non-dual source—has seniority over cosmic fields particulate "points."
16. Habituation: rational automaticity to achieve selective focus to produce effects. Mishabituation: assuming false purpose/identity with irrational, compulsive habit/attitude/behaviors. Dishabituation/deconditioning ... erasure of sub-rational automaticities through focused dialogue.
17. Absurdity-realization with "relief." End-phenomenon of giggle paths dialogue cycle ... realized absurdity is pretense of not knowing revealed.
18. Mental pictures as having actual spatio-temporal location; are created but with lesser density phenomenon.
19. Re-contextualization, as rational symbol/word reframing, with consciousness of abstracting restored in dialogue.
20. Problems: subjective vs. objective (quasi-equivalent sub-rational fixed or balanced stasis contrasted with free flow of intention within a rational gaming opposition context).
21. Psycho-Psych/Holosophy: differences.
22. Productivity/Morale relationship as dependent on actual VFPs (valuable final products) identified and achieved.
23. Synonyms as blurred distinction channels of "word-identity" rationalization of sub-rational behavior.
24. Holon as puppeteer versus puppet of all mental/brain process.
25. Capacity for SM/selective memory searches require cognitive fore-knowledge enabling recognition of memorial image.
26. Responsibility versus blame: Mis-emotional attribution of cause (blame) with personal causal participation denied.

27. Error-Limit template for rational limitation versus its pseudo "Karmic" implanted success reluctance copy.
28. Success reluctance as redundant sub-rationally imposed "memory" of E/Limit game constraints.
29. Delegate/Dump as counter-productive managerial avoidance.
30. Sub-rational/Illness: Psychosomatics 70% of all illness as tension-based.
31. Connection to unethical sources cause Illness/Rollercoaster (loss of gains) and all dis-ease causation by stimulating the success-reluctance need to convincingly not handle a challenge to restore ability; being victim "proves" not a villain.
32. Proactive versus reactive: Free choice versus stuck in past with false-belief domination of awareness.
33. Cosmos/Material Universe/Multiverse/Megaverse/versus a consensual Kosmos.
34. Existence = combined conceptually (knowings made manifest as a four dimensional/cognitive combination).
35. VFP (Valuable Final Products) actual defining cycle of worthwhile, useful, productivity.
36. Cycle of Action: basic projected unit of spatio-temporal actualization, e.g., (be-do-have or begin-continue-complete) in Cosmos.
37. Ideal Scene as rationally imaginal goal or aspiration.
38. Entitlement Mentality/Privilege "owed to," versus Earned/Intra/Entrepreneurial having as productivity.
39. Deferred Gratification/Suspended Disbelief/Rationally Selective inattention, (Thralldom as rationally believable continuity; game-serving pretense).
40. Density discrimination as degree of willingness (ability) to perceive with certainty, solidity of appearance.
41. Rational survival as volitional and purposive doing, versus mere existence at effect.
42. Eight Domain Kosmic Ethics (full multi-domain objective calculus) versus mere Cosmic situational ethics.

43. Hidden Standard as sub-rational "losing" or odious comparison preventing direct perception and communication of subject necessary for erasure.
44. "Analysis" Paralysis … "look don't think," … solves it …
45. Token Performance/Product/false pretended, misrepresented achievements.
46. Sub-rational counter-Intentional/Doubt-Liability-Enemy attitudes as specific descending levels of negative, emotionally frozen, destructive and compulsive activity.
47. Ethics levels as index of degree of sub-rational judgment and behavior domination, i.e., codified levels of sub-volitional counter-productivity.
48. Self versus Other Determinism, i.e., degree of true self-actualization.
49. Trance versus Thralldom, "Illusion/delusion" ratio: trance as sub-rational thralldom or reality distortion by imposition of past.
50. Self-actualization/authentic witness/confront/communication restoration of holon's primal non-material view point and actualization.
51. Potentiality → Know → Source → Create → Cause/effect, primary epistemic hierarchy as infinite potentiality descending to Knowing … etc.
52. Top-down causation: Future and Imaginal Motivation as senior non-material causation of all unfolding eventuality.
53. Confrontability: sustaining personal presence — hold position/composure/equanimity despite any challenge or stress.
54. Holon ultimate cause over RM/Selective unawareness/sub-volitional susceptibility as covert causation.
55. Jung/GPM/Ancestral Memory/Archetypes as Primordial, and Universal Gaming Templates.
56. Pre-optimization stages defined as gradient levels of confidence restoration.

57. Ripple effect, post-erasure expansion cycle: cognitive "reverberation" (unforced extension of any cognitive implication or resonance).
58. SM as redundant duplication of Life-Game with displaced command value to "survive" as enforced continuity of its installed pictured copy.
59. Systematic erasure as linking thread to basic case-contour erasure/dissolution of complete implanted actual-pattern duplicate.
60. SM is a duplicative mental-image mockery of error-limit to erroneous pictured "survival" and time-bound "computation loops," of compulsive behavior
61. True character versus case-contour (its sub-rational pictured copy).
62. Conceptual thought as instantaneous (imaginal) versus pictorial thinking (persistent time-bound mental imaging).
63. Communication as gradual and remedial distancing from, = with the restoring capacity to convey honestly, and directly witness, necessary to erase.
64. Symbol definition: "Meaning Mobility Mass" a reified combination of conceptual elements but distinct from what is represented."
65. Sub versus unconscious versus preconscious (about to be conscious).
66. Holon demo ... Directed mentally picturing reveals holons actual distance from any redundant pictures projected. (Dramatization = no distance.)
67. Ideal consultant/presenter based on Holosophic principles of communicative intentionality, and data-mastery.
68. Connecting versus relating: mere correlation is not causation (e.g., thoughts versus brain states).
69. By-passed charge = sub-aware triggering contact of traumatic material without relief of erasure or cognitive closure.
70. Resisted disclosure or withhold = triggered concealment without disclosure and resulting charge (Tension).

71. Warranted Assertability as useful degrees of properly assigned truth-values.
72. Preliminary optimization levels as outer shells of core case-contour "charge" removed in counseling; "onion peeling."
73. Essence/Existence: conceptual prioritization required for rational judgment.
74. Kosmos versus Cosmos ... Kosmos adds and includes seventh and eighth domains.
75. Re-framing as extended multi-contextual knowing released and expanded from a fixed memorial "knowing-about."
76. Eight domains as holoarchy: General sub-rational "charge" experienced as emotionally and painfully disordered, conflicted, and "cumulative" mental-emotive energy within and between domains as (organized system) holoarchy.
77. Emotion as "felt" mental-energy bridging thought to action.
78. Concepts as "knowings" or abstract meaning versus "information" as a process of numbers/symbols meant to convey meaning.
79. Observer-participancy: potential/probability conversion to event by conscious choices by an observer.
80. Zone of irresponsibility: influence denial; pretended sub-volitional and unknowing causation, to avoid admission of cause.
81. Life energy as high wave-length entelechy (purpose-driven, i.e., telic, non-material source) directed by consciousness to produce cosmic effects.
82. Re-stimulation as sub-rational response to challenges requiring ability increase — resulting triggered Success Reluctance as ability and ultimate revelation restraint.
83. Mental creation exceeding maximum-considered confrontability, results in sub-rational solidification of a confront-perimeter to restrain further ability-increase (SR).
84. Panpsychism: all material events as subjects (holons): i.e., all is mental.

85. Transformative acceptance as willing and full acknowledgment of what is; followed by erasure and novelty as rational progressive change.
86. Telic — purpose in action — an intentional coming into existence.
87. Ontic-pertaining to being as existence, primal actualization.
88. Noetic: epistemic, pertaining to knowing about.
89. Selective unawareness as the epistemic gateway from seventh to sixth and extending domains.
90. Polysemous, as multi meaningful.
91. "Conscious of abstracting" awareness of contextual signification; necessarily requires a selective cognitive choice of specific meaning from an infinite abstract contextuality.
92. Retributive reflex as sub-rational guilt requiring compensatory suffering.
93. Capacity is not compulsion: all capacity when fully restored is rationally choiceful therefore optimal (good in degrees).
94. Zero-sum versus more rational multi-sum game in which every player wins something.
95. Gradient scales as specified degrees of change of quality or quantity in any universe.
96. Resist versus counter as rational opposition without blaming or sub-rationally motivated opponency.
97. Optimization as a "Calculus of Betterment" in degrees of graduated goodness tending toward an Ideal.
98. Reify: endow with, substance, or degrees of "solidity."
99. Agency: a unitized spiritual being, a conceiving individualization or postulator of perception. The Basis problem: why does awareness (if material) have a private cognitive boundary and is not smeared out through the universe as are material wave-lengths and particles?
100. The Binding problem: why are perceptions not quantified as discrete physical "dots" or quanta but perceived as cognitive wholes?

101. Compulsion as hidden "value added" sub-rational demand input that distorts optimization calculus.
102. Kosmic reality as volitionally subtracted occasions of playfully displayed knowing from an infinite cognitive potentiality.
103. Cognition as selectively revealed pretense of not knowing.
104. Causation as distinct from correlation, e.g., brain → mind.
105. Evaluation (told what is) (versus indication (pointed to what is) in counseling.
106. Affinity as a scale descending from an infinite co-existence potential for realized Being.
107. Reality as a scale descending from a primal consensual and projectable co-experiential agreement.
108. Communication as creation accessing a mutually infinite context.
109. Qualia ... projected and cohering percepts creatively subtracted from infinity into meaningful substantiation.
110. Charge ... painful emotion that is life-energy in tense, functional dis-harmony
111. Benevolent recreational display as primal Kosmic purpose.
112. Cognitive inference as rationally accessed future certainty.
113. Induction/deduction → rational reduction of staged un-knowing.
114. Erasure expands context sensitivity to selective novelty.
115. Cognitive cascade as an expanding awareness perimeter.
116. Compulsion as sub-rational volition.
117. Fixed idea as belief with false sub-volitional premium.
118. Familiarity: selectively relevant un-pictured knowing, which enables the rational advance into novelty of life-gaming experience.
119. Meta-narrative as descriptive dialogue producing an expansive implication of alternatives.
120. Retro-causality belief putting effect preceding cause, e.g., mentally pictured past causing "present" perception.

121. Singularity: the minimally manifest limit of cognitive potentiality, i.e., zero point of emergent finitude, also a point of minimally selective appearing (must obviously be conceptual).

122. Event horizon as the variable-seemingly permeable perimeter of a "black hole" . . . or primal cognitive gaming barrier?

123. Knowing point versus viewpoint: One must be first able to know in order to look ... conceptuality is senior to and enables its projection as any combined conceptuality or act of envisioning, i.e. perceiving of reality.

124. Optimization: intentional improvement or incremental increase of qualitative or quantitative betterment of any sub-optimal situation or condition by volitionally adding: 1) exact, accurate, and full knowledge; 2) increased control of any sub-optimum situational aspects or lack of intent; 3) expanding awareness of personal and ultimate responsibility for any committed or omitted action re situation; 4) ensuring that all incremental betterment includes reference to the maximum number of domains when implemented.

125. Universe definition: 6th domain; full extent projection and content of any personal plus consensual awareness and viewpoint; extended view points that are primarily agreed to by all holons; the volitional appearing of an independent scenario; a perspective caused by a mutually habitual expectation; a presentational immediacy of combined, meaningfully projected, and shared agreements; substantiveness as apparent novelty-specified; a reified, enduring and consensually shared construct of combined conceptuality or Qualia.

126. Universes (Types of)
    - Home • Created • Multi-dimensional
    - Multiple • Finite • inflationary (evolving)
    - Serial • Infinite • Recurrent
    - Earlier • Expanding • holographic

- Bubble • Parallel • Lilac (consensual)
- Baby • Cyclical • Simulated (artificial/computer)
127. Telomeres: The protein caps at the ends of the chromosomes which help them from deteriorating or shortening a major factor in aging and disease. They operate in the same way as the caps on shoelaces keeps them from unraveling, Telomere length has been sustained and even restored nutritionally, and by various spiritual counseling modalities.
128. Reconcealment: sub-rationally uncommunicated (discreditable) eventuality repeatedly concealed … an important target for erasure.
129. Intention can mean more than its philosophic definition as mere "reference to." It is defined in Holosophy as the capacity to cause, focus, and bring into being; or as the degree of ability to usefully actualize a goal.
130. Thralldom: the capacity of the holon to "self-enthrall" i.e., to rationally self-convince, bemuse, or provide a workable illusion sufficient to achieve a momentary absorption in an engrossed goal of playerhood.
131. Core Blame: The basic implant engineered blaming -postulate which provides as perpetually rationalized and re-enacted, the primal impetus for sustaining and reinstituting a sub-rational false copy of the Kosmos. It forms the primal oppositions, *under duress*, with core misemotional countering of any apparent life game-revelation and erasure. The *copy* made to falsely restore the game *is* the sub-rational mind, and contains that core irrational blame for needing to be replaced.
132. Happiness/success: the ability to endow, perceive, pose, and resolve problems and attain related goal; to rationally survive with consistent display of increased quality of life across all 8 domains of Kosmic existence.
133. Cognition Corridor: The communication pathway or

cycle that undeflected or distracted, leads inevitably to revelation and erasure; giggle path; comm-conduit, et al.

134. Erasure: Erasure is essentially the volitional cessation of post-traumatic mental picturing. More fundamentally, it's the directed *true* self realization of the holon which restores its actual perspective as a *non*-material individuality without *past* encumbrances.

135. Singularity*: a theoretical region in space and time in which all the forces of nature collapse to a point of infinite density from which a new universe emerges. Also in philosophy, the creation of a super-intelligence to benefit mankind. (see also 122)

136. Pain: (1) The body's natural warning sensation of injury or disfunction. (2) Since that warning is *perceived* as sensation it can also be memorially copied as a mental image and re-imposed on the body *from the past.* (3) Such *re*-imposition is very convincing until its *sub*-rational and self-punitive origin is perceived and fully realized. (4) Upon such realization the apparency of *past* pain being real and in the present is *erased*, and the sub-volitional need for pains *suffer*ance and all *un*natural *psycho*somatic limitation ceases to be created.

137. Are quarks conscious? Holosophy favors "agentive Cosmopsychism," the view that the universe itself is conscious *in degree*, from a cognitively *knowable* and therefore experiential "nothing" or *absence of*, to an endowed and projected gradient scale of cumulative awareness.

---

*Holosophy may have additional special usage for many of these terms which are explained in page notations as introduced and applicable.

Appendix X

Origin of Life and Information - Some Common Myths (*excerpted*)

In previous articles, I described the thermodynamic challenges to the origin of life, and I explained the need for information in the first cell to originate from an outside source. Now, I will dispel many of the myths associated with attempts to circumvent the information challenge.,

A common attempt to overcome the need for information in the first cell is to equate *information to a reduction in entropy* often referred to as the production of "negative entropy" or N-entropy. This connection is in certain contexts justified by the fact that both *entropy and the Shannon formulation for information* use the same mathematics and can be related to probability and uncertainty. For instance, this approach can be used to calculate the amount of work required to *generate specific amounts of information in the amino acid sequences of proteins*. However, entropy is not equivalent to the information in cells, once the latter represents *functional* information.

> To illustrate the difference, imagine entering the kitchen and seeing a bowl of alphabet soup with several letters arranged in the middle as follows:

> ## "Rest today and drink plenty of fluids. I hope you feel better soon."

You would immediately realize that some intelligence, probably your mother, arranged the letters for a purpose. Their sequence could not possibly be explained by the physics of boiling water or the chemistry of the pasta.

To continue the analogy, you mention your design inference to your friend Stanley Miller the Third who happens to be an origin-of-life chemist. Stanley believes any attribution of design to pasta sequences in soup is based on the concerned-parent-of-the-gaps fallacy, so he mocks your superstitious beliefs. He then states that the sequence could have come about as a result of the boiling soup cooling to room temperature.

Since cold soup has a lower entropy than hot soup, he believes the reduction in entropy could have generated the information in the message. You would immediately recognize that a reduction in thermal entropy has no physical connection to the specific ordering of letters in a meaningful message. The same principle holds true in relation to the origin of life for the required sequencing of amino acids in proteins or nucleotides in DNA.

A related error is the claim that biological information could have come about by some *complex systems or non-linear dynamics processes*. The problem is that all such processes are driven by physical laws or fixed rules. And, any medium capable of containing information (e.g., Scrabble tiles lined up on a board) cannot constrain in any way the arrangement of the associated symbols/letters. For instance, to type a message on a computer, one must be free to enter any letters in any order. If every time one typed an "a" the computer automatically generated a "b," the computer could no longer contain the information required to create meaningful sentences. In the same way, amino acid sequences in the first cell could only form functional proteins if they were free to take on any order.

Moreover, protein chemists have determined that the vast majority of sequences in proteins today are *indistinguishable from being purely random* which further confirms that those in the first cell also appeared random to first approximation. Any relevant divergence from pure randomness would have been due to constraints associated with protein folding, such as the formation of a-helixes. To reiterate, no natural process could have directed the amino acid sequencing in the first cell without destroying the chains' capacity to contain the required information for proper protein folding. Therefore, the sequences could never be explained by any natural process but only by the intended goal of forming the needed proteins for the cell's operation (i.e., *teleologically*).

Brian Miller, Mathematician

Appendix XI

Belief frames and causes perception and behavior...
Charged belief compels *irrational perception and behavior...*

The mind's ability to contextualize or to frame raw perception by belief* is what actually constructs our ordinary life experience... where this experience is unknowingly re-framed by belief-responses to the painful events of the past, the result is, as we have discussed, unnecessary and aberrant limiting of ability and awareness...to illustrate the importance of a free and unencumbered contextual or interpretive framing capacity, try to 'solve' the framing of the figure above and identify its subject... For the missing constructive background 'solution' and some other examples of the mechanisms of framed seeing... 'See' the following page...

---

*By observation and text, sub-rational (traumatic) experiences can frame and distort belief and that such "forgotten" belief influences and can sub-rationally command irrational perception and behavior.

Duck / Rabbit

Old Woman / Young Woman

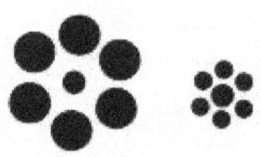

Center Dots are The *Same* Size

Eskimo / Indian

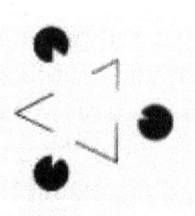

A Triangular Nothing?

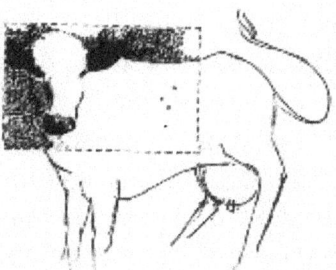

The Picture Pasteurized

Appendix XII

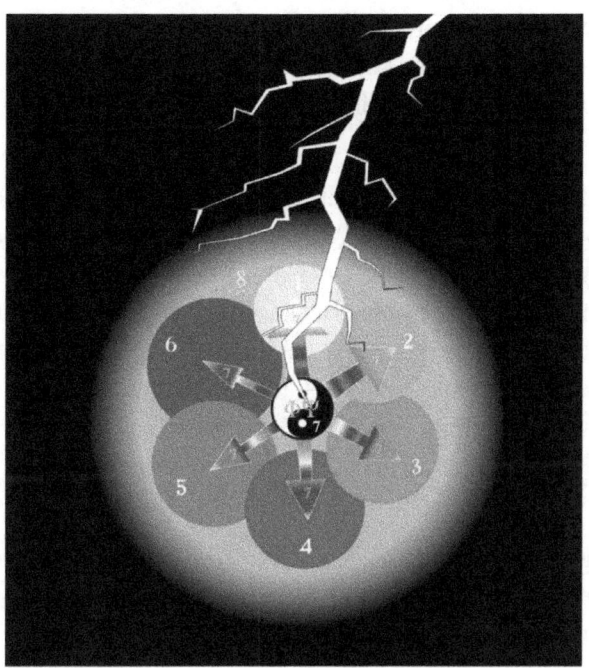

The Fateful Invitation:
A Cosmic Fable

Let's consider a fanciful, perhaps instructive, narrative that presents an illustrative but apocryphal history of "pre" historic post traumatic conditioning or inculcation ... i.e., the implant mechanism.

...A very able and as yet not embodied holon with elected feline propensities happens upon an obscure planet in a distant galaxy populated with mouse-embodied holons.

With uber-feline curiosity and playfulness, the "cat" begins to "play" with some of the planetary mouse inhabitants with injury and occasional mortality occurring. The Planetary Council of Mousehood, in an emergency session, takes up the matter. After much further cat-ish deprivation by our feline predator, and no practical defense solutions forthcoming, the Lord of the Primal Mouse Council suggested a drastic remedy.

It is decided that the mice will, as a nation, pray to their cosmic ancestral source for guidance. Meanwhile, at the distant edge of the cosmic game-in-progress lurks an alien invader force seeking a dominant entry into the cosmos. Because the invading aliens haven't entered the cosmos at its consensual beginning, they weren't part of that *initial endowing* aggregation and thus, haven't paid their *primal* and personal game perpetuating "dues," and are, therefore, unable to directly and physically enter the local "cosmic" game-in-progress.

The general Kosmic capability which endows and enables *all* games enables the mice's cry for help to be received extra-sensorially by the aliens waiting at the perimeter of the cosmos. (A cognitive reach of sufficient magnitude, focus and direction, crosses all universal barriers and perimeters since those very strictures are ultimately sourced from above and beyond any combined material barriers.)

"The Word of God" is handed down by the aliens telepathically to the beseeching mouse suppliants as "answered prayers," incorporating a "divine" plan of action to "restrain" the cat, but actually to establish indirectly a conquering increment of influence by the aliens over a universe the lurking invaders couldn't otherwise connect to or effect directly.

Divine Commandments for Mouse Salvation (English translation)
I.   Sub-rational thinking consists of the memorial image-making of the past ... as distinct from conceptual or imaginal thought, which

is immediate, evanescent cognitive novelty, and the instantaneous emergence of the actual ... sub-rationality cloaks the resulting rational choice-making, which actualizes and optimally gives value to Kosmic play.

II. An explosion site is to be baited with large clustered or aggregate numbers of sacrificial and embodied mouse holons.

III. Additionally, and most crucially, a generic but accurate image of the active game pattern of existence will be telepathically projected into the blast scene to be copied *under duress* by the feline-entity.

IV. This will be perceived by the unconscious (but still with rudimentary awareness and capacity) feline-entity as a prohibitive and destroying revelation of its game sanctioning and enabling *selective unawareness* (consensual Thralldom)

V. The traumatized feline, even under extreme duress, is an immortal and ultimately creative being. It's *intra*-traumatic, *sub-rational solution* to the apparent prohibited and revelatory erasure of the total Life-Game, is to make an instant *replacement* mental copy of the seemingly revealed actual game-pattern to *salvage* its enthralled cosmic continuity.

VI. Upon "recovery" from the implant-trauma, the aware but now subtly influenced feline-entity will continue to compulsively endow the false copy of the life-game it copied memorially to mistakenly sustain its original consensual obligation of total self-entranced Life *Game participation*.

VII. That now post-traumatic and self-enthralled game endowment is accompanied by false self-limitation with artificial restraint of harming (SR) and copied impulses to "survive" with limiting ability to *view and erase* the restraining game-copy!

VIII. The feline's self-limiting of behavior and ability is now artificially imposed *and justified* by synomymic mis-definition basically self-implemented by using the hidden (and attached) co-implanted mouse holons with selective unawareness to *appear* as its own limiting thought process and motivation.

VIII.   This begins an implanted dwindling and deceptive spiral of success reluctance, false opponency (blame) and general installed disability successfully distracting the feline adversary of the mice from further destructive impulse and activity.

Thus the mice "solved" the marauding and lethal playfulness of the Cat, but at what ultimate cost to themselves and future descendant cosmic populations? The aliens gained a "foot in the planetary door" with vast unprecedented influence for contagious aberrant and therefore evil dominance of our galaxy. Thus began an enduring cosmic peril, to be constrained only by an enabled awareness of the true nature and source of the *sub*-rational ... and an informed dedication to fully reveal and defeat ... and *erase* it.

Fin

Appendix XIII

True "Self" Trancendence

∞

No meditation on any kind of object is helpful. Meditating on an object, whether concrete or abstract, is creating duality ... meditate on what "you" are ...

∞

The thought Who am I destroying all other thoughts will itself finally be destroyed, like the stick that stirs the funeral pyre.

∞

The Sage is never other than the real self of the disciple ... When that self is realized, there is neither guru nor disciple.

∞

Without ego, there is no karma ...
I am that by which I know I am

Ramana Maharshi,
Yogi Contemplative

See "Holosophy: Restoring the Souls Code
Chapter II for further discussion

Appendix XIV

> True meditative practice and the transcending idealization of Art and Value are the metaphoric celebration of, and ascendant access to the Sublime
> Holosophy Canon
> Do not equate Serenity with incapacity
> Ancient proscription
> Among the great things which are found among us, the *existence of nothing* is the greatest.
> Leonardo DaVinci.

Paradox as Meta-Logical Order

Discussed below are the variants of both the *manifest and reconciled* duality aspects of Paradoxicality, referencing the background of an ultimate* conceptual order. Such an order provides a final reconciliation of all apparent variability of *displayed awareness* projected from a boundless infinitude of potentiality.

Paradox: Meaning and derivation from cognitive Order:

All paradoxicality is derived from a *concealed*, but potentially manifest meaning and order. A paradox is a seeming contradiction of "conflicting truths," a statement which has at once a (6th domain) context as a substantive, verbally represented fact, but, at the same time, covertly references a hidden *non*-material meaning (7th domain). This is done without making a true distinction between the two different, irrationally superimposed, but *un*equal, and *domain -distinctive* frames of reference! Combining the two without true *domain differentiation is* the source of the paradox, e.g., *"I"* am lying... or "this" statement is false ... or ... Does "the barber" who only shaves those who don't shave themselves ... shave himself? Or, people who are tolerant reject intolerance, therefore are themselves intolerant of intolerance - a "true" but *conflicted* "self-referencing duality. Similarity unwanted conditions (fixed ideas, equal and opposing intentions with resulting mental tensions and

---

*Reconciliation is here defined as a *working interaction* of varying degrees and aspects of a specified thing with the *necessarily* and implicit defining *exclusion of all else*.

dilemmas) result from this seemingly paradoxical equivalence resulting from a post traumatic *indistinction* between 7th domain conceptuality and 6th domain physicality ... between meaning and referent, and/or between an imposed post-traumatic *memory* and an undistorted perception of actual fact. A *targeted realization,* in dialogue, is the distinction and erasure of the aberrant traumatically produced equivalency of past and present, mental-image with actual perception... the persisting illogic of domain *in*distinction, as an imposed and copied 6th domain *image* of a misplaced 7th domain *conceptuality*!

Meta-Logical *non*-duality as the cognitive source of *all* Logics:

Logic is a multi-valued *symbolic variable,* selectively applied. Logic itself doesn't *explain* logic. Only an *external* ultimately higher cognitive capacity which itself *is the source of logic* provides the transcendent Kosmic conceptuality that is senior to, and resolves any apparent formal *symbolic* contradiction or *illogic*. For instance, the philosophic tradition of "sufficient reason" (everything has a prior cause) is sanctioned only by the binding logic of the *Cosmos*, its rigor does not apply in the 7th and 8th Kosmic domains wherein anything can be, or *not* be, *for any reason,* in any time frame, or within *any* chosen location or imagined perspective! This necessarily pre- or *meta*-cosmic potentiality for the specified agreements is required for the *agreed to preceptual complicity* of all holon-players in the Kosmic game. Thus, the innate unconstrained meta-logic of non-duality (the 7th domain) is *reified* and consensually projected (6th domain). Accordingly, the substantive, *and subtractive* logic of duality, i.e., a *something* (+) enabled and actualized by the selective *absence* (-) of everything *not* that thing, produces an instantiated and enduring fabric of novelty and play ... the Kosmos!

Scale of Duality-Integration by Domain:

VIII: Neither one nor many - as *Itself,* but is an infinite *non*-dual *potentiality* for all specification of knowing.

VII: The one *and* the many, an unlimited *variably combined* (differentiated and associated) *conceptuality*, with projection *potential*, but not yet projected.

VI: The one is now actualized by consensual exclusion from the many. The cognitive combination capacity (height, length, width, and variability of form) together with the variable (something/nothing) duality ratio projected, provides a domain of common substantive (material)constituents. A *playing* field with a variably evolving/devolving spectrum of co-active players extracting play/opposition capacities from higher domain duality-*potentials,* and enacted as *cosmic* probability and eventuation.

V–II: To fully project and optimally manifest a complete inter-domain game exchangeability of rational, orderly play-activity, the Kosmos is *differentiated* by type of *domain integrity* (distinction of type of game cycles, exchange purposes, and *oppositions*). The total modality of progressive dualistic* novelty, *or thralldom* (rational pretense) is thereby perpetually endowed and made manifest as Kosmic Play.

---

* Duality here manifests as the mult-domain functional frame and player-perspective of the *individual holon* (persona). This is the enabled viewpoint of each holon, a unique *window* of Kosmic player participation. This dualistic (I vs. all else) integration of each holon capacity is a non-material source of both postulation and perception (its unique creative universe-projection). Thus duality is *constructively* enacted (6th domsin), but not yet ultimately *reconciled* as the essence of a gaming opposition, playfully and kosmically displayed: A transcendent beacon of infinitude (7th domain) projected and made manifest *as* game, or a benevolent Kosmic recreational display.

Appendix XV
The Persisting Problem as Hidden Paradox

To further explicate the basic mechanism of all hidden, aberrant domain displacement let's consider the *subjective*, or apparently *in present time*, problem; as a persisting but *un*wanted life-condition or circumstance. Such a problem is falsely perceived as *perpetually immediate*, a continually *present* threat or concern; a seemingly *un*wanted effect or *worrying necessity*, experienced as *current*, persistent, and protested by the Holon.

This apparent fixed location in an uncomfortably persisting "present time" of an unwanted state of existence is caused, as is the perception of any fixed dilemma or "paradox," by the hidden but compelling confusion of the 7th domain's innate, unprojected *conceptuality,* with the 6th domains *materiality*.

That primal intentionality of all Holons, to endow and preserve the life-game, is deceptively copied, and displaced, *under extreme duress*. This occurred during an ancient cosmic trauma which seemingly threatened total life-game-continuity with destructive interruption, or erasure, by a *forced revelation* under extreme duress. The intention was, by imposing a traumatically-installed game-revealing deception, to force the targeted holon to mistakenly, and *unnecessarily* recreate, or "restore" the selective-unawareness of self and group *entrancement* necessary for game continuity. The primal and actual pattern of game-existence, which each player-Holon has a transcendent commitment to perpetuate, was seemingly threatened with revelation, and like any trick revealed, would lose its vital *game endowing capacity* to enthrall and convince.

The 6th domain playing field (physical universe) is essentially a rational and substantive conditionality enabling the primary play activity of inter-domain exchanges (i.e. specified and particular exchangeable; *somethings* derived selectively from an infinite range of potential possibilities). However as explained, during the "ancient cosmic trauma," an intentionally imposed or implanted copy of the game-pattern itself was mistakenly re-created by the Holon to "save" it from a premature and game interrupting disclosure. This further imposes the implanted deception that a total game-destroying revelation is occurring and must be "solved" or prevented by a redundantly *re*-created, and preserving , i.e. copied and *re-concealing* image of its primal game-template, The actual life-game play-consensus remains continuous and essentially inviolate because it was never at risk through the forced revelation of any single Holon!

The post-traumatic (implanted) result is a sub-rationally imposed mockery of the normative eventuation and novelty of the 6th domain. This is analogous to the symbolic paradoxicality of scientism, or strict materialism. In philosophy, the "present time" problem (paradox) compulsively (and unknowingly) imparts a mentally pictured representation of reconcilable duality* *from the 7th* or conceptional domain and, in a mockery of the actual pattern projection, imposes it substantially on the 6th. This *simulation now compulsively appears to*, prevent the Holon's awareness (and rational erasure) of the pictured substitute, as not being the original life-game.

The apparent solidity and fixedness of the "present time" problem is now revealed as merely a sub-volitionally extracted *copy, or imposed reflection* of the 6th domain gaming potentiality inherent in the *7th and 8th* domains... The apparent conditional and *balanced fixedness* of the "present time" problem is a *displaced* mental *copy* of the as yet *un*projected duality-potential of the higher, transcendent, domains.

---

* As discussed in the previous appendix, reconciled duality is the 7th and 8th domain potential for the actualized, projected, unreconciled duality of the 6th (something vs. nothing, in degrees) that allows specificity and projects and endows the consensual agreements of the *Real*...the spaces, matter, energy, and time of the 6th domain playing field.

A higher cognitive example of *reconciled* duality derived from a "paradoxical" knowing*ness* above mere specified projection of the *symbolic* is, e.g. "neither the one *nor* the many." These higher non-material paradox-perspectives, when copied under a traumatic *implanting duress* and then falsely projected as an authentic and actualized 6th domain (material universe), become the redundant, falsely balanced and persisting duality of the 7th domain's *mental copy of the 6th*; and then "perceptually" *reimposed as the false and persisting conditionality and stress of the "present time" problem!*

This *present* problematic apparency is actually a stressful *substitute* overlaying the hidden pseudo-cosmic equivalency and intent of the true *balancing potentiality* of a senior, 7th domain intentionality not possible in, or native to, the physical universe! (When this false *equivalence* is seen, and realized in counseling, the Holon ceases to "creatively" impose it as a sub-rational, and seemingly fixed 6th domain, *mental image-substitute*.) The persisting or "present time problem" is now seen as an imposed "balanced" *redundancy*, and *erases*, restoring the actual physical universe pattern of *novel non*-equivalent and the ultimately *un*balanced 6th domain *motive* intentionality, necessary for cosmic games of opponency and rational play.

As referenced in earlier analyses of paradoxicality, the fundamental difficulty is in *not* definitively separating the 7th domain (conceptuality) from the 6th (physicality). A *subjective* or "persisting" problem exists "physically" *only* as falsely superimposed *mental imagery*; as a fixed and seeming equivalence of intent; a deceptive game-pattern replica *extracted under duress* from the conceptually idealized (universal) to falsely equal the physically (particular) and substantial. The resulting false equivalence and unwanted problematic conditionality is a deceptive, and persisting conceptually *balanced* image of intentionalities displaced from the 7th domain and imposed as a "present" problematic stress on the 6th. Note that the apparent unwanted problem condition is itself *not in the physical universe*, but the Holon projects its aberrant "balanced intentionality" newly as a physical copy to maintain the seemingly threatened (by implanted revelation) life game. So it is this residual game-preservation intentionally and sub-rationally reimposed as false game revelation* barriers and success-reluctance** that "forever" requires a life-game distorting imposition of a *compulsive* and deleterious *substitute* unknowing which, is the ultimate cause of all aberrant suspension of the rational continuum and integrity of Kosmic Play.

*An apparent paradox in quantum theory is the "measurement problem", which seemingly requires *consciousness* to resolve the randomness of the cosmic background into a "collapse" of a single state of existence...a *living observer* halts that cosmic randomness! Things exist in *all* possible forms until a conscious observer "freezes" that randomness into a single, finite state, i.e. *the collapse of the wave function*, which describes the probability of an existence occurring in *any* particular state. Our perception of reality therefore stays stably projected as a reality as long as *consciousness is involved* as the projector! With that creative observer-context in mind, as a *Kosmic* referent, *any* injected revelation of the total games' *conditions*, e.g., *full* disclosure of intent, origin, or prematurely restored awareness of the *consensual thralldom* making a zero-sum and *game-ending conclusion* a certainty. To falsely and sub-rationally prevent or avert this premature revelation is apparently the prime and *implanted* motivation for *all* aberrant unknowing and disability.

** Success Reluctance as the problematic and sub-rational physical displacement of normative consciousness and ability is the final (overriding) determinant in the holon's obsessive and transactually injected effort for *unnecessary* self-limitation, and game replacement.

To accomplish this, it uses the sub-volition mental imagery of a traumatically installed compulsion to *copy for* preservation, the seemingly threatened (by forced revelation) continuity of the holon's volitionally enthralled *un*awareness of the *actual pattern,* of the life-game. This persisting and rationally pretended unknowing is the vital selective unknowing necessary for this, or any, game's continuity. All objective (real world) problems require unequal internal intent vectors to permit solubility, i.e., there is no *fundamental* equivalence in the physical universe, therefore no typical cosmic problems can ultimately contain a fixed (equal and opposite) purposiveness or intentionality. The sub-rational *subjective* problem is therefore an additive *mental construct* compulsively imported from the 7th (conceptual) domain to provide a *mentally pictured and memorial success-reluctant* obstruction to the holon's rational, and *normative* cosmic (6th domain) ability and awareness.

Present problematic imposition on consciousness essentially results in the impairment of ability to separate the 6th and 7th domains required to *rationally* distinguish and thereby exchange fungible content between all domains. The sub-rational replication of the *game in progress* under extreme duress, provides the *solving game-copy*, which is then sub-volitionally endowed as *actual,* to mistakenly prevent its dissolution by *enforced* revelation. The resulting *problematic reluctance* to rationally create cosmic-game novelty and thereby discard the aberrant copy, is the seminal essence of all aberration.

Appendix XVI

Kosmic Archetypal Triads
Core Existential Templates

Be	→ Do	→ Have
Begin	→ Continue	→ Complete
Create	→ Survive	→ Destroy
Affinity	→ Reality	→ Communication
Truth	→ Goodness	→ Beauty
Start	→ Change	→ Stop
Plan	→ Implement	→ Result
Subject	→ Verb	→ Object
Possible	→ Observation	→ Real
Order	→ Entropy	→ Chaos
Cause	→ Distance	→ Effect
Space	→ Energy	→ Object
Differentiation	→ Association	→ Identification
Quality	→ Relation	→ Quantity
Plus	→ Neutral	→ Minus
Source	→ Existence	→ Condition
Concept	→ Combination	→ Appearance
Idea	→ Intentions	→ Action
Potentiality	→ Possibility	→ Actuality
Actuality	→ Agreement	→ Reality
Singularity	→ Projection	→ Entropy
Past	→ Present	→ Future
Birth	→ Growth	→ Death
Possible	→ Observable	→ Actual
Essence	→ Choice	→ Existence
Presence	→ Transition	→ Absence
Observe	→ Evaluate	→ Decide
Notice	→ Duplicate	→ Erase
Image	→ Item	→ Entity
Field	→ Wave	→ Particle
Energy	→ Condensation	→ Solidity
Semantics	→ Syntax	→ Semiotics
Self-determined	→ Other-determined	→ 'Pan'-determined
Condensation	→ Compaction	→ Concretion
Thesis	→ Anti-thesis	→ Syn-thesis
Non-Duality	→ Duality	→ Paradox
Play	→ Error	→ Limit
Instantiation	→ Alteration	→ Continuity
Freedom	→ Purpose	→ Barriers

Appendix XVII

Holosophy Publications

Holosophy: Restoring the Soul's Code Volume I (Revised)	Metaphysics of Consciousness Series Number I
Holosophy: Exploring the Kosmic Code Volume II	Metaphysics of Consciousness Series Number II
Managing by Statistics Volume I	Introduction to Management Series IV Number III
Problems and Paradox (in progress)	Metaphysics of Consciousness Series Number IV
The Transformative Dialogue: Remedial Markers, Aphorisms, Prescriptions & Principles	Metaphysics of Consciousness Series Number V
The Holosophy Dialogue Protocols (With appendices)	Metaphysics of Consciousness Series Number VI
Success Reluctance: An Introduction to a Basic Element of Human Aberration	Metaphysics of Consciousness Series Number VII
Ethics and the State of Optimum: Gradients of Rational Behavior	Metaphysics of Consciousness Series Number VIII
Sub-Rational Indicators: Emotion, Attitude, and Sensation	Metaphysics of Consciousness Series Number IX
The Case for Immortality: (A Research Supplement)	Metaphysics of Consciousness Series Number X
The Case for Consciousness and Its Survival of Bodily Death (A Research Supplement)	Metaphysics of Consciousness Series Number XI
The Sub-Rational Synonym List An Inventory of Mis-defined Word-Triggers of Irrational Behavior	Metaphysics of Consciousness Series Number XII
High Wisdom Quotations (Holosophy Information Supplements)	Metaphysics of Consciousness Series Number XIII
Kosmos vs. Cosmos: The Case for Intelligent Design and A Darwinian Revisioning (A Holosophy Information Supplement)	Metaphysics of Consciousness Series Number XIV

www.ingramcontent.com/pod-product-compliance
Lightning Source LLC
LaVergne TN
LVHW061310060426
835507LV00019B/2086